ISSUE BASED TEE

MON

BY STEPHAN

Published by
Scripts To Stage
www.scriptstostage.co.uk

A CIP catalogue for this book is available from the British Library.

BookPrintingUK
Remus House
Coltsfoot Drive
Peterborough
PE2 9BF
Telephone: 01733 898102

ISBN: 978-1-912541-20-1

Printed and bound in the UK by BookPrintingUK

Website: www.bookprintinguk.com

A monologue is a long speech made by one actor. Monologues appear as a large chunk of text on a page and can seem intimidating. These tips will help you deliver a structured and confident performance.

- Read your chosen monologue.
- Break the speech down into smaller chunks. This will help you memorise the lines and really understand what the character is saying and feeling.
- Read through the monologue and separate it into sections. Mark with a pencil any changes in thought, topic or emotion.
- Now think, is the character sitting, standing or a mixture throughout the monologue?
- Once all this work is done, then it's time to learn the lines.
- Practice the monologue vocally. Act the monologue out in many different ways: standing, sitting, running, lying on the floor, skipping etc. This will enable you to be able to perform as the character in the monologue more naturally.

WHO AM I?: FE/MALE TEENAGER

I've grown up not knowing. Not knowing who I am. I'm not saying I've got a bad life. I've got a very good life. My mum and dad give me everything, sometimes too much. But there's always been something, something I've wanted to know. Who I really am. I go to a private school and the kids from home make fun of me. They tell me I'm spoilt, tell me I'm lucky, that their mum and dad are struggling. They tell me that they can't afford to go to some stuck-up school and that's when I want to scream at them, I want to shout, at least you know. At least you know who your parents are. I don't know what my biological parents look like, I don't even know their names. I don't know if they work or if they're even dead or alive. I mean, I know my mum and dad of course but not my real biological parents, not the woman who gave birth to me or the man who created me. I've never even seen a photo of them, but it's my secret. I'm ashamed. I'm ashamed to be adopted. I live with the shame of not knowing. The shame of not being wanted by the two people in the world who are supposed to love you unconditionally no matter what you do. I know I'm lucky to have such a loving, caring mum and dad but I still feel that shame deep in me. That shame that if those who conceived me couldn't love me, how can anyone else? I'm ashamed of them, my parents. I'm ashamed they created me just to give me away. Give me away like a loaf of bread to a neighbour, or worse, a stranger in the street. I was that unimportant they gave me to just anyone who'd have me and no matter what school I go to, or what I get for Christmas, that still hurts. It still hurts when I look into my mum's blue eyes with my biological brown eyes. It still hurts when we visit the doctors and he turns to my mum and asks if we have a family history of that illness. And she turns to me and says we don't know. That's all I ever want, to know who I really am.

THE MOMENT: FE/MALE TEENAGER

It feels like I've been working all my life to get to this moment. *Results day*. I think I did ok, but I can't be sure. I did my best. Yes, I definitely did my best. Mum and Dad keep telling me that as long as I tried my best, that's good enough for them. Oh, but what if it's not good enough for me? Anything would be good enough for them because they have absolutely no ambitions. They both hate their jobs and moan about work, but when I ask them why they don't find new jobs they just tell me they're lucky to even have a job. Why are they lucky to have a job they hate that hardly pays the bills? Why don't they want to do better? What if I can never escape this estate because all I'm good for is working in a dead-end job like Mum and Dad. Getting up every day, moaning, going to work, coming home, moaning and going to bed. I couldn't stand to think that was going to be my life forever. I dream of doing things and seeing places, but they're not interested. They always tell me, 'we're happy here and as long as we've got each other that's all that matters.' But I'm afraid that's not all that matters to me. I want more. So, I've no pressure from Mum and Dad to do well, but they are the main reason I want to do well. To me, these results are like the difference between having a life or living a mundane, monotonous, existence like Mum and Dad.

I DIDN'T WANT TO BE HERE: FE/MALE TEENAGER

I googled how to kill myself. The first thing that comes up is the Samaritans number. I didn't want to talk. I didn't want to be here. I just wanted it all to end. I had an ache inside my head that was stabbing at my emotions. It was itching at my self-belief making my body crawl with contempt for itself. It felt like a thousand hands of strangers touching my skin as I flinched. Flinching to get away from the unease but everywhere it touched me. I just felt like a burden. Insignificant. No one would miss me and if they did, they'd be better off without me. I wanted to know what the most successful method was, you see. I'd screwed up at life, I didn't want to screw up at dying. I'd fail at that too like I fail at everything. That's what stopped me in that moment. I didn't want to contact the Samaritans to be one of those lonely people who have no one to talk to but some pious, patronising do-gooder on the end of the phone. That was my problem, I didn't talk. I didn't tell anyone. I didn't want to bore them. I didn't want them to feel sorry for me. I didn't want them to tell me it'd be ok. I just wanted to get out of my mind, to rest, to be at peace. Well, before I knew anything the tablets were in my mouth. I was swallowing them, swaying in and out of consciousness and I woke up here. I was right all along, just like I fail at everything, I failed at suicide. I'm still alive. Mum found me unconscious. I was rushed to A&E and they realised I couldn't move anything except my left arm. I was sent for scans where they found I had a spinal cord injury. They think it was caused by the severe drop in my blood pressure. No movement from my shoulders down. They hope I'll see improvement. I hope I'll see improvement. I'm still trapped in my mind but now I'm trapped in my body too. But I woke up to see the sunshine and my other worries seemed so insignificant. I smelt the freshness of my aunt's perfume. I tasted the sharpness of the orange. I felt the kiss of my mum. I heard so many kind words. I've had so many visitors and cards from friends and family. People I never realised truly cared. I was never alone. I just chose to be. If only I'd spoken to one of them, maybe even the Samaritans, anyone, maybe I wouldn't be in this hospital now. Maybe I wouldn't be relying on other people to wash me, feed me and dress me. I really can't run away now. I have to face up to everything.

YOU'LL NEVER BELIEVE: FEMALE TEENAGER

This is so funny, honestly you are seriously going to wet your knickers. The party on Saturday at Louisa's was hilarious. I laughed all of Sunday and this morning, didn't I, Dana? OMG, I so did. Anyway, talking of parties, where the hecky fecky were you? No, don't tell me, were you having a nice romantic time with Spike? Anyway, I forgive you for leaving me all on my Jack Jones. Well listen, the goss is that Helen only went and tongue twizzled Jonathan Scuttler. Oh yes! Well, the story goes he was upstairs snogging the face off Sophie Marshall in the bathroom, I mean, well gross and so unhygienic in the bathroom. Well, Helen finds out and belts upstairs and all we can hear is her shouting and swearing at Sophie Marshall. Obviously, there's history there babes, you know what I mean? Anyway, this is the juicy bit, Jonathan falls out of the bathroom and I'm telling you he was well gone, when Helen grabs him, falls on top of him and starts snogging his face off. The poor lad didn't know what to do, he could hardly stand. Everyone was on their phones taking photos and videos. I'm telling you babe, you missed a brilliant party. I bet you're well jel.

GROWING UP DIFFERENT: FEMALE TEENAGER

I don't know how I ended up at private school. My mum lost custody of me when I was only seven. At school I was accepted, I suppose, but I always felt like a fraud, like I didn't really belong here with all these stuck up kids with parents with flash cars and big houses. I was as intelligent as everyone, more so than most, so I didn't feel different in that way, but I just didn't feel like I belonged, I just felt different. I did get on with a few of the girls, I mean they weren't all from families with loads of money. Some were quite down-to-earth, and we could have a laugh, but I just couldn't settle. I just couldn't find my feet. I had too much going on in my life that most of them could never even imagine, so I kept a lot to myself and to top it all off I'd come to realise I was gay. It's like, can't you just give me a break, life. I just want to be normal. Truthfully, I was lonely, isolated and lost, so I started being disruptive. I couldn't control my temper and if the teachers said anything I didn't want to hear, well, I just couldn't be bothered, I'd just leave class. I'd walk out. The school didn't really know how to cope with a case like me. I was quite a unique pupil to them. I was always being told to report to the headmistress and in some ways I quite liked being told off. It was the only time I really had one to one attention and it made me feel important, like I actually mattered in the scheme of things. I never had any money, so I started sniffing glue. It was the cheapest option and after seeing my mum's battles I didn't really want to end up addicted to hard drugs. This seemed the best option. Took the shine off my worries slightly and got me noticed. I used to go back to school after all the other pupils had gone home and sit on the steps with my head in a plastic bag full of Uhu, hoping a teacher might come out and try to stop me, and give me a bit of attention. One day I was sat outside school about four-thirty and the deputy head, Miss Lumley, came out. She noticed me straight away. I'd been sent to her office several times, so she knew me pretty well. She didn't shout or threaten me with detention; she just sat down next to me and listened. I'd always liked her, but it was like she knew what was wrong, she just put me at ease. For some reason I told her everything, how I felt. Maybe it was the glue. I even told her I was gay, and she didn't flinch, she didn't bat an eyelid. She just put her hand on my shoulder and told me it'd be fine. She said she could relate to my feelings, nothing more, but I think it was her way of telling me she was gay too. I might have been wrong, she never confirmed it. She played a big part in making me feel I could just be liked and accepted for being me. It was a little less worry in my world.

THAT'S MY PART: FEMALE TEENAGER

Have I just heard right? Lucy Collins has the main part in the senior show. I must be having the worst nightmare ever. Lucy halitosis-breath-Collins has the part I've been wanting my whole life. What do you mean, I'm only thirteen? I know, and for at least the past ten years I have watched *Grease* every week. I am Sandra Dee. That part was written for me. I even had a holiday romance at the beach with a boy called Danny. Louise Baker, he told me his name was Danny and I believed him, ok? Well, I'll have to text Mum and let her know and I can tell you she will not be happy as she made the largest donation to the drama department last year to guarantee me that part. I'll have to cancel my blonde highlights at the hairdressers, oh this is not good. I mean Lucy Collins has ginger hair as well, so she'd be perfect playing Cha Cha. Right, there has got to be some mistake. No, I'm sorry I can't accept that halitosis, ginger minger Lucy Collins is a better actress than me. What am I going to do? I'm going...I'm going... to pull out of the show. Yes, that's what I'll do and then see how they feel. What's that Louise, no that can't possibly be right. You'd better be joking around. They've put me as stage manager. You cannot be serious.

BEING THAT GIRL: FEMALE TEENAGER

We'd been going out for almost two years. I really fancied Jake from the moment I saw him. I never thought he'd be interested in me. When he asked me out, I tried to act cool but inside my heart was doing loops. And it was great at first, well, I thought it was still great, then he dumped me. I guess he'd been a bit distant for a while, I should have seen it coming but I didn't expect him to be so hurtful. He was nasty. He called it off, blocked me, he wouldn't get back to me. We finally met up and he told me one of the reasons he'd called it off was because he felt like he was kissing a guy because I had a moustache. He told me my eyebrows were like giant caterpillars and that I'd put on weight. It was blow after blow. I mean, only a week ago he'd told me he loved me. He really messed me up. I haven't eaten properly since. I was too embarrassed to tell my mates or anyone. I just cried to myself and looked in the mirror thinking, well, he was right, I do have big eyebrows, a moustache and I am fat. I hated myself. I hated the way I looked. I needed to take action. I found some of my mum's hair removal cream and rubbed it all around my mouth. After about fifteen minutes I realised it probably wasn't the best option. My eyes wouldn't stop watering, it stunk, and it left a red patch all round my mouth. Not an improvement. I moved on to my eyebrows. I sat in my room plucking for what seemed like hours before getting the nail scissors and giving my brows a trim. I think I went too far. I had to get my mum's eyebrow pencil and attempt to even them up. I tried to convince myself they looked alright and my red mouth was looking a bit better, although really, I knew I looked like a reject TOWIE star. I'm just so unhappy. I've tried so hard, I've made so much effort to try and be that girl, look like the girl that Jake wants, but when I saw him yesterday he looked at me like something he'd stepped in, called me names to his mates and walked off with his new girlfriend. I'm more of a mess than ever and I've still not got Jake back.

GONE VIRAL: FEMALE TEENAGER

I've known Mark for years, since we were in primary school. His family treated me like one of their own. We holidayed together, I trusted him, he was my best friend. Everyone used to say we were boyfriend and girlfriend, but I'd always tell them, no, we're more like brother and sister. We moved to secondary school and again we were put in the same class. We'd hang around in the same gang and go to all the same parties. I ruined everything when I started seeing one of his friends, Dave. Things seemed a little weird at first, but he said he was cool with it. Weeks passed and he seemed to change, he appeared distant and we stopped sharing and talking like we used to. I just put it down to the fact we were getting older and growing apart. Things started to get more serious with Dave. Mark knew we were getting serious and started to make sly comments to me. I don't think he realised just how much they hurt me. The night of the party everyone was there, and we all got so wasted. I don't normally drink, but everyone was. It was Annabelle's party and her parents were away. We were all partying so hard and well, one thing led to another and I ended up going upstairs with Dave. Everything seems a blur, but I know one thing: we had sex. I know it was really irresponsible. What was more irresponsible and unforgiving was Dave got his mates to film us. I would never have known, except for the fact it got posted online. How stupid was I ever to trust him? I can't believe I trusted him, and he betrayed me. All those plans we had, gone up in smoke, and I really did love him. Dave denied everything, he said he knew nothing about it.He blamed Mark, he said that Mark was so jealous. I really don't know who to believe. All I know is complete strangers are seeing my intimate parts and the whole school is laughing at me. How low could they go? I trusted Dave. Mark was my best friend. I just don't know who I can rely on or trust anymore. I've been betrayed.

EVERYONE'S WAITING: FEMALE TEENAGER

Today's the day, it really is. After all these months of planning, it's finally here. I really don't know how I should feel. I can tell you though, I'm not feeling anything at the moment. What's wrong with me? After all these months of planning, the endless chat, the excitement building up and now, nothing. Oh no, I can hear voices, I can hear everyone outside arriving, all gathering around and chatting to one another. Mum and Dad are rushing around the house like headless chickens getting everyone refreshments. The noise in my head is starting to gather some sort of momentum. Oh no, not now, please, not now. Right, grab the middle of your hand and breathe, close your eyes and think of nothing. Come on, you can do it. Oh no, I think I preferred feeling numb, please, not now. Where's the paper bag? Or any kind of bag, although not plastic. I don't want to breathe in toxins. I read in an article about killing the planet, that plastic bags contain toxins, well, some only small amounts but still you have to be careful. Oh, for goodness sake, I just want a bag, any bag, breathe. Oh no, not yet, the cars have arrived, please not now. I really don't think I can face this just yet. Right, breathe and remember saying goodbye to people isn't forever. They'll always be there in all the memories you've shared. Make them proud and enjoy life at college and university and become that doctor you always talked about. Right, I'm almost there, oh, come on feet, put one in front of the other. Once you're in the car it'll all be ok, all your friends will be there and Matt will be at your side, the gorgeous boy who asked you out before anyone else in the school. Why did he ask me out? Was it for a laugh? Does he even fancy me? Oh, I really don't think I can go. I know what Mum'll say, 'don't be so silly, everyone's waiting outside. If you don't go, you'll regret it for the rest of your life. When I was your age, I never had the opportunity to say farewell. We just left school and started work.' Come on Carla, put one foot in front of the other. Prom night's a memory you'll treasure forever.

I SHOULD HAVE BEEN A BOY: FEMALE TEENAGER

They were always saying *she should have been a boy* when all I wanted to do was play with my brother's toys. When every week I used to cry at dance class. When all my friends were boys. *She should have been a boy* they laughed, as I tried to teach my twin sister to wrestle and gave her a bloody nose. It was a joke then. They said it in jest. It wasn't a statement that scared them. It wasn't a statement that made them cry. It made them smile. They said it without a second thought, with affection. They said it as they stroked my hair, as they hugged me tight, as they smiled at me with pride, as they went about their day. It was just the way I was, and they loved me for it. The thing is they were right. I should have been a boy. I could feel it. I knew I was in the wrong body. Every fibre of my body yearned to be inside a male exterior. I felt male, but when people looked at me, they perceived me differently. It's only chromosomes and pronouns, I know. Why does it matter so much? But to me it had become everything because it all felt so wrong. I wanted to have hairy legs, short hair and wear boxer shorts. I should have been a boy. They looked at each other and clenched their hands. They cried and they questioned, *are you sure you're not just a lesbian? What difference will it make if you become a boy? How will changing your name help?* It's about identity. It's about representation, but no matter how I explained they couldn't understand. They didn't want to understand. I didn't want to be their little girl anymore. I wanted to be me. I wanted to be recognised as me. It was how I felt. I can't explain it. It wasn't a choice. It's instinctive, like some people like the taste of honey and some people don't. You just don't. You don't need to justify why. You don't have to find an explanation. It's just the way it is. This is the way it is. I instantly became a stranger to them. I felt like I was trying to fill the shoes of someone I could never be. They didn't recognise me anymore, they said. All I'd done was repeat the words they said so often as I grew up. I should have been a boy. It's a horrible feeling when those you love the most can't accept who you truly are, and I need them now more than ever. Before it's too late. I'm trying to be brave. I'm trying to transition and although it feels so right, it's not easy. I want them to support me, welcome the real me to the world. It's not easy at all. Every day at school I get the unoriginal taunts, the insults, the pushes and the shoves, just for being me. I just want to go home and feel accepted, loved and welcomed, but I don't. I'm ostracised, just like I am at school. There is no let up wherever I am. Wherever I am I'm alone. I wish they could just remember how it meant nothing to simply say she should have been a boy. I wish they could walk in here now and repeat those words *you should have been a boy* and laugh and smile just like they did when I was younger. Stroke my hair, hug me tight. But they won't. Will it matter what sex I am when I'm not here? Will they miss me wearing a dress, will they miss me not dancing, will they miss me not playing with dolls, will they miss my long hair, my breasts, my periods? Will they? Will they? Or will they miss my personality, will they miss me? The me they never truly met. The me they never gave the opportunity to exist.

FEELING GROWN UP: FEMALE TEENAGER

We still couldn't believe it, that we'd been invited to Josh Hutton's eighteenth birthday party. All the sixth form kids were there and there was so much booze. We'd never been to a party like it before and we were only fifteen. You wouldn't believe the house. Josh's house was amazing, it was like a mansion and so posh. Like, on the way the taxi driver was telling us what footballer lived in which house. I think Lauren felt like a right WAG. To be honest, I felt like it was something out of an American college movie. It all seemed so exciting. Well, we got inside, and I got separated from Lauren and found myself wandering around this dream house trying to find her. I ended up in the pool area, can you believe it? A pool area. Everyone was drinking and throwing each other in, it was crazy, and then I felt a tap on my shoulder and when I turned around Matt was standing there. Matt was Josh's best mate and they did everything together. Matt asked if I wanted a drink. I remember feeling really embarrassed after I said I'd have a Fanta and he smirked and asked, do you want jelly with that? I laughed it off and said, no, vodka, and I can remember him smiling and saying, 'yes, that's what we like.' I ended up sitting chatting to him for what seemed like ages, well, until one of the older girls came across and said, 'Matt, which children's department did you find her in?' I remember him telling them to stop being cruel and walking off with them. I sat by the pool for a little longer and I think I finished my drink. I remember seeing Lauren across the other side of the pool but as I got up to go over my legs gave way. My head was spinning and then everything just went blank. The next thing I remember is lying on a bed with loads of coats on top of me, trying to get up but my legs felt like jelly. My clothes were all on back to front. I could hear voices. I recognised the voices. It was Lauren and Josh and Matt. As I came round, I remember watching Josh and Matt leave and I remember asking Lauren what had happened. She said I'd fainted, and so Matt and Josh had helped me to a bedroom, but when they went to leave, I'd thrown myself at Matt. I couldn't remember anything, she said, 'you must remember.' I started to cry. I just couldn't remember. I didn't know how I'd ended up there. I didn't know why my clothes weren't on properly. I was so upset and so confused and all Lauren could say was, 'you manage to bed a gorgeous boy like Matt, and you don't even remember it, how drunk were you?' I didn't sleep with him. I didn't sleep with him. I'd only had that one drink; I couldn't have been drunk. What's wrong with me? What's happened? I only had one drink, honestly. I only had one drink. I wouldn't – but Lauren insisted I was up for it. I just wanted to go home, I just wanted to go home. I wanted to get out. It didn't make sense. I'd had one drink. I remember saying to Lauren, *I must've been drugged. Matt must've put something in my drink* and Lauren told me not to be silly and that no one would ever believe me. I'm sure I must've been drugged – and raped. But Lauren just didn't want to know. She seemed to think it was all some kind of joke, a laugh. I just feel sick. I just want my mum.

I HOPE SHE WAS WORTH IT: MALE TEENAGER

You were my best friend. We always played out together when we were young. We were on the same football team, walked to school together and played out every night. People used to say we were glued together. At fifteen we'd sit and dream of what car we'd drive, where we'd live, how many kids we'd have. We shared everything from football to our amazing dreams. Then it happened, she happened, and you changed. The girl changed you. We'd arrange to go out and you'd cancel, because your girlfriend didn't want you to leave her. She never liked our friendship and the gang never saw you anymore. Why would you do that? Why would you put a girl before us? I hadn't seen or spoken to you for months, you started to avoid me in school and then we ended up at the same party. What made you decide to come that night? I'm not sure you were even invited, so what were you doing stood in the corner holding her like some crazed lunatic, as though she'd escape if you let go? I didn't mean to follow you both upstairs, it was a joke. The lads thought it'd be funny to walk in and ask you if I could join in. It was supposed to be funny, a joke. We used to have a laugh; say we'd share anything. Your face changed. You didn't look happy. I was drunk or I'd have told the others to stop egging me on. But I did it. I asked if I could join in and you saw your arse, your face changed and you chased me down the street and on to the park. I tried to calm you down, but you were having none of it. Your eyes were crazy, you lunged at me with a knife. I couldn't believe it; it was my knife. The knife I gave you the last time we went fishing. But you carried on. There was blood everywhere, I begged you to stop but you continued, thirty-six times you stabbed me. You carried on until your hand couldn't stab anymore. You left me to die, on a cold, damp, blood-soaked floor. Your best mate, your brother. I hope she was worth it mate.

ON THE RUN: MALE TEENAGER

My name is Elijah and for as far back as I can remember I knew I was different. As a child we moved house so many times, sometimes I'd forget where we lived. I changed schools with every move and to add to my disjointed life I was abused by my mum's boyfriend, that's my half-sister's father. I became so angry and disruptive and I hated the world. I couldn't tell anyone though, even if I'd had the courage or someone I could trust. Who would ever have believed me? At the age of eleven I was already known as a troublemaker. Other children didn't want to hang around with me or were told by their parents not to. I was the one not invited to any birthday parties or sleepovers. I'd be called names like weirdo, freak and later much worse. I couldn't turn to anyone. I'd made my own bed and I had to lie in it. Mum's boyfriend left and she started to drink more and more, and I had to take on the responsibility of looking after my sister. I made sure she didn't get ridiculed. I was determined to look after her and protect her. Some nights we'd have no food and as we had no money either, I went and stole from the local supermarket. I did everything to keep us together. I washed and ironed our clothes and made sure she felt safe. Mum, well it wasn't her fault. She'd disappear for days and when she came back, she'd physically and verbally abuse me. I wasn't bothered. Whilst she was hitting me at least my sister was safe. Then one night everything changed. I can't believe how stupid I was. I got caught stealing and when Mum was nowhere to be seen we were both taken in to care by children's services. We were both put in to a care home and I felt like a caged animal. We should have been safe there, but who would have thought that this was going to be the start of our problems. They said we'd be kept together, well, that was the first lie and then they said we'd be safe, lie number two. My sister was placed in a foster home but with my reputation they couldn't take me. They said I'd be placed in a special home with someone who had the right environment to look after me. I overheard one of the workers, I'm not sure who, call me damaged goods. Well, if that's what they think then that's what they'll get. My temper got worse and I'd end up in major fights and, of course, there were lots of meetings about me. Ben was one of the workers at the care home.

He was nice, he always took the time to talk to me and ask how I was, but he left soon after I started to trust him to get another job. Charlie was the cook and she'd often let me help her in the kitchen, but then was given a warning for health and safety and putting a minor at risk. The world's gone mad. That's when I decided to leg it, get out of there, disappear. So, I took my opportunity one day when I'd finished school. I'd put some clothes in my school bag and away I was. I didn't know where I was going or what I was going to do. The world had become an open space and I had to fill it. I got a lift off a lorry driver and my adventure, good or bad began.

BUT I LOVED HIM: FEMALE TEENAGER

My name, it doesn't matter. It used to, but that's when I felt something and now, I don't feel anything. I drink. I drink more than I should until I feel out of it and I'm a different person. I'm happy for just a few hours but then I wake up the next morning and I'm still me. I wasn't always like this. I know, that's what everyone says but for me it really is true. I used to like myself, have friends, but that was before I met... him. So, I started seeing him. I thought he was lovely, good looking, loads of money. I used to think how lucky I was, and all my mates were so jealous, especially when he collected me from school in his sports car. They never said so, but I could tell in their eyes. We'd go for pizza and he took me to parties. He'd buy me dresses, make up, you name it, and take me shopping loads. On a Friday night he'd give me vodka and cigarettes and I felt well grown up. All my mates would be round at each other's houses and I'd be partying till the early hours. Mum didn't know what day it was, let alone worry what I was up to. She was out of it on anything she could get hold of, booze, drugs, in fact she'd smoke the garden lawn if she could. I used to say that's why Dad left us, and she'd say it was my fault because I was such a little bitch. So, when he told me he loved me, that was it. He loved me and that's all that mattered. My friends told me I should be careful, he looked older than he said. He told me not to listen to them, that they were just jealous. Told me I should hang around with him more. He said they were so immature, even told me that my best friend tried to come on to him whilst he was waiting for me. I wanted to confront her, but he told me to leave well alone. I believed everything he said. Life was amazing, he was so sweet and loving...but that all changed. We were going to this party at one of his mate's and he was all on edge. I'd honestly never seen him like that before and I kept asking him what was wrong, but he said he just had some financial worries, he blamed it on me. Anyway, we arrived at the party and after a few drinks he told me his friend really fancied me. I thought he was joking. Well, without going in to too much detail he owed him some money and he'd spent so much on me lately he couldn't pay. He said if I loved him, I needed to make his mate feel special. I really didn't know what he meant. He sent me to talk to him, but it was really hard 'cos we had nothing in common. He was really old, even older than my dad. Then my boyfriend came over. I thought he was going to rescue me, but he said his friend wanted to sleep with me. I refused and he grabbed me really tight, he scared me. He said if I didn't do it, he'd get beaten up really bad. Well what choice did I have? I was only fifteen, but I loved him, and I didn't want him to get hurt. So, I did it...it was horrible. It didn't last long and then my boyfriend drove me home. He said he loved me, and I'd done him proud. I didn't feel very proud. I got home and I cried all night. What had I done? But then I remembered my boyfriend's words. He loved me and I'd done him proud. I thought that'd be the end of it and everything would be fine. It wasn't.

IT'S ONLY A STUPID PHOTO: MALE TEENAGER

Phone beeps.

(*Reading text on phone*) You're giving me no option.

Phone beeps.

(*Reading text on phone*) I'm only asking one thing.

Phone beeps.

(*Reading text on phone*) I can't deal with you.

Phone beeps.

(*Reading text on phone*) You are determined to make me do this.

Pauses to respond.

I will do it; I'm not just saying it. I'm going to have to. You leave me no option. I've had enough of you now. I've asked you nicely, I've told you. This is the only option I have left.

Pauses to text.

See what you've done now.

Phone beeps.

I knew that'd get your attention.

Phone starts beeping constantly.

All you had to do was send me a video. You teased me with the photo and then when I say I want more you go all shy. Well you're not being shy now. Your naked selfie is flying around cyberspace and into every inbox.

Looks at phone.

Seems people like what they see, like I did.

Phone starts ringing.

(Scoffs to self) Huh, knew that would make you want to talk to me. It's all a bit too late. I did warn you. All you had to do was send me a naked video and it could have been just between you and me. You sent me the photo when I asked you, you didn't need much persuading to do that. I did genuinely like you, but I just wanted you to do what I asked and the more you said no, the more I wanted it.

Phone keeps ringing.

You can wait now. I've waited long enough. The lads are loving this.

Answers phone.

For crying out loud, what's the matter? What do you mean? Everyone thinks you look great, like a bit of a slag, but great body. Get over it. I did tell you what I was going to do. I gave you plenty of warning. Keep your wig on, it's done now. Should have done what I asked then. I did say that would have been just between you and me. You're glad you didn't, why? Are you enjoying all the attention? Everyone warned me you were a slut. Most of the lads have probably already seen it before. Phone the police. What will they do? Give me a caution. Everyone can't unsee what they've all seen. So, it's illegal, you're under eighteen. I'll just tell them we're a couple and you're over sixteen anyway. Of course that makes a difference. I didn't force you to send it me. A paedophile? A paedophile? Are you serious? How do you work that one out? You sent them to me. I won't go to prison. It's only a stupid photo. Even if I take it down it's still out there. I did warn you. What? You're threatening me now. Ok, I'll take it down if you just send me a video. No, I wouldn't put that live. It'd just be between you and me, like I said in the first place. Only take you two minutes and I'll delete the photo from everywhere. It's not too late. Loads of people won't have seen it yet. So, are you going to send me one? You don't know! Why, do you like the idea of everyone ogling over your photo? Who are you going to ask for help? Your mummy and daddy? Bet your dad will like seeing his little girl starkers, Herbert the pervert. Ok, ok, sorry. Just send me a video and I'll take it down straight away. Do you think I want everyone perving over my girl? It was the only way I could get you to talk to me about it. Go on baby, just do this for me and I'll take it down. Most people will never even know it was online.

THAT TIME AGAIN: FEMALE TEENAGER

I really didn't want to get out of bed this morning. My head was banging, and my stomach was really sore. Mum said I'm becoming a hypochondriac. I asked her could she spell that, and she said that if I can be sarcastic then I wasn't poorly and should get ready for school. I told her that if I collapsed and fell in front of a bus, she'd feel so guilty. Mum just tutted and said to hurry up or there would be no bus to fall in front of as I'd have missed it. My mum has no sympathy for anyone who is sick. So, off to school I went, and I felt hot, sweaty and dizzy. I headed straight to the toilets and thought that's the best place if I'm actually going to be sick. So, I took up my place on a chair next to the sink. I never would have thought what a busy place the girls loo would be. I sat there and people would come and go and tell you odd stories. Some would come in and leave because I was sat there, and they felt embarrassed and then Miss Smith came in and asked why I was there. I told her I was feeling sick and she said, 'Faye, is it your time of the month?' I was like, what's she going on about? My face must have looked puzzled. Miss Smith said 'Faye Powling, are you on your period?' I told her I'd never had a period and she looked confused and just left. Well, to be honest what business is it of hers? It's a bit personal, don't you think?

TOO INTENSE: MALE TEENAGER

Kyle and me had been best mates since primary. We both got into Moorside and we were well chuffed we'd still be at the same school. We used to joke around in class and sometimes got into trouble but nothing too bad. We were about thirteen when Kyle started getting a bit obsessed with all the girls. They all fancied him, but I think he was a bit full on, stalkerish, and it put them off. One girl, Amy, didn't seem to mind and it all got intense really quickly. He didn't want to bother with me anymore. They seemed happy together...but they were literally always together to the point where we all used to take the mick out of them. Kyle didn't seem to care and neither of them really bothered with anyone else anymore. I'd message Kyle, go and knock for him, but he wasn't interested. He never got back to me or said he was too busy. When I did speak to him, he just seemed a bit weird, and he was always looking around for Amy. I just thought he'd proper fallen for her. He told me he loved her after about a week. I'd never been in love with anyone. He said I didn't understand, and if I'm honest, I didn't. He just seemed boring. He had no interest in anything but Amy. I'd see him in the corridor and jump out on him and he'd just flinch and turn away. He didn't see the funny side anymore. It was like I was too childish for him now he was all grown up with Amy. I started hanging around with my other mates more and just got sick of bothering with Kyle. I feel a bit guilty now, I suppose. I should have known something was wrong. It was all way too intense. I should have tried to get him out more, stop him spending every minute of every day with her, but like I said earlier, he'd always been a bit full on with girls. A bit stalkerish. I just thought it was his way and him and Amy both liked it being full on. I saw him a couple of times and he looked like he'd been in a fight. I asked him about what he'd been up to. He'd just shrug, change the subject and ask if I'd seen Amy. I just thought he'd had a fight with someone 'cos they'd been eyeing up Amy. I presumed it was him being jealous. It never occurred to me it was her. I mean, he was taller than me, much bigger than Amy. He could handle himself. Through school he'd always stood up for me. He was the hard one. I was proper shocked when I heard he was in hospital. His mum told me. She called round to ours. She told me what had happened, how they'd been worried for a while. They'd heard Amy shouting at him. They'd noticed how he didn't have his friends around anymore, how he didn't go to football practice anymore, how they were always together. They thought it'd fizzle out. It was just a teenage crush. They didn't expect to come home and find him battered and bleeding in the front room. Amy wasn't there, she'd gone. His mum said Kyle couldn't keep it in anymore. He cried like a baby, she said. He told her everything. She'd broken his arm, pushing him down the stairs. I went to visit him. He had to have it pinned. He said she hadn't meant to do it, but I think she probably did. I didn't say that to him. Everything made sense though now. The reason he'd flinched in the corridor, it wasn't because I was too childish, it was genuine fear. The scratches and bruises. Why didn't I realise? He wasn't the jealous, possessive one, it was her all along. He opened up to me and showed me some of the texts she'd sent him. She'd even told him to stop seeing me. He was so embarrassed, so ashamed. He looked defeated and I was so ashamed I hadn't been there for him. I just didn't even think he'd be getting hurt. I just thought it was normal for some people to get so loved up they didn't want to see their friends. I didn't really think about it. I was just upset he didn't want to be my best mate anymore. Some best mate I turned out to be.

NO DREAMS FOR TOMORROW: FE/MALE TEENAGER

Skank, stoners, smackhead, baghead, king bong, druggie, crackhead, losers. Off their heads and out of hope. No life, no aspirations, no dreams for tomorrow, they all just get by, beg steal and borrow. What life is that? Drug dens and crack houses, tin foil and spoons, lighters and smoke, scoring to get high and deals to live by. The only things that matter. The only things these people care about. I don't get it. I never want to be one of them. My childhood hasn't been great. I've seen it all. I've been part of it. Used as a decoy, a safe bet. Who'd use their kids to score? Who'd use their kids to make a deal and get away with it? You see, that's why I want to be different. I want to be better. I want to do more. I don't want to be like my family. People say, *make your parents proud*. My parents don't actually have any emotions, they're dead behind the eyes. They wouldn't be proud if I ruled the world. The only thing that'd make them proud was is if I was a druggie or a dealer. They might even love me if I could supply them. It's not easy though, trying to get out of this cycle. Sometimes I could easily give up, it'd be much easier to just become one of them. To join the lost race, to not care about getting anywhere in life except high. I often think it'd be great to escape this world and then I remember the come downs, the way it made them treat me, their lack of respect for themselves, the shakes, the desperation for a hit. The fact that drugs become the only thing in the world before friendship, family, loyalty, love, and I don't want that. I definitely don't want that. I don't want people calling me a skank, a stoner, a smackhead, baghead, king bong, druggie, crackhead or loser. I don't want to be off my head and out of hope. No life, no aspirations, no dreams for tomorrow, just getting by, having to beg steal and borrow. I don't want that.

RESPECT TRADITION: FEMALE TEENAGER

Mum and Dad were arguing again last night, and I feel so guilty as they're arguing over me. Don't get me wrong, Dad's not a tyrant or anything, he's just got his beliefs and, well, I suppose he wants to stick to them. I think Dad feels like he's losing control. Lately, all I hear him saying is, 'women don't act like this. What would your grandfather say?' Well, not to be disrespectful but times are changing and, well, lives and religion need to change too. Dad accepts modern culture, well, kind of, but he wants us to respect tradition and the old-fashioned religious values too. Mum, on the other hand, wants us to be like every other girl, to have freedom and to choose a life for ourselves. I think that's why Mum was so upset when Dad announced he was taking me abroad in the summer holidays to see family. Mum knew exactly what that meant. Dad had found me, his eldest daughter, a suitable husband. I don't know what to do. I don't want to upset my father, I don't want to disown our faith and traditions, but I'd like to be able to choose the person I am going to spend the rest of my life loving for myself. That's why they are constantly arguing. Mum doesn't want me to go and have an arranged marriage and Dad says she's disrespecting his decision as the man of the house and, well, my opinion isn't even asked. I don't think I'm even supposed to know the plan. I think they think I can't hear them. This has been going on for weeks and there's only two days left until the summer holidays and, to be honest, I'm getting really worried, I'm scared. I don't want to go. I don't know what to do. Should I tell someone, a teacher even? Maybe I should just tell Dad I don't want to marry a man chosen for me, a man I've never met and wouldn't have more than two weeks to get to know. Maybe I should just be truthful and tell my father I don't want to get married, well not in the traditional way, anyhow. Oh, this is going to be so hard and if I tell them I think I'll probably lose my family for good. The problem is, well, it's not really a problem, just a different way of life, you see I don't want an arranged marriage, or any marriage to a man. I practice in my head everyday what I'm going to say. *Dad, please listen, I am in love and that's why I can't marry the man you've chosen. Maybe one day I'll get married and I'm not sure what you'll find worse, the fact my love isn't of the same religious background and beliefs as us, or the small detail I've failed to mention, that I'm going to spend the rest of my life loving a woman.*

I NEVER SAW ANY DIFFERENCE: MALE TEENAGER

We shared everything. You stayed at my house and we'd play on X-Box and PlayStation, or whatever latest gadget was out. We'd eat pizza and drink Dr Pepper and have belching and farting competitions. Our life seemed so simple; or so I thought. We'd meet in the holidays with all our school friends at the park and ride our bikes, play rugby and go for lunch at the chippy. My mum used to ask what we did all day and I'd say *nothing much*. The days of the summer holidays seemed to fly past and we were moving into another year at school. We had all these choices to make, options of what career path we were going to take. My interest was in sport and that started to take over. I was training most nights and at weekends. I didn't realise you were feeling so lost. I thought you'd hang around with the others, but they didn't seem to want you without me. You should have told me. I saw you as my best friend, but they saw you as someone from a council estate with a mum struggling to keep one step ahead of the debt collectors. I didn't realise they called you a skank and the rest or else I would have stopped them. I didn't notice much. I was so privileged, wrapped in cotton wool and obsessed with football and rugby. I never saw any difference in us, you know, but looking back I always wondered why you'd always ask to stay at mine. I could never understand why you'd want my old clothes I'd grown out of. You'd say it was because they were designer, but I didn't even notice the labels. You should have come on that holiday with us, it wasn't much fun with the other lads, they didn't know me like you did. They all said you didn't have the money to come, you were poor. It's nothing to be ashamed of, in fact it makes you stronger, well, that's what my auntie says. I came to find you when we'd got back but you'd gone. I didn't understand, why didn't you say something? The neighbours said they had no forwarding address for you and you'd gone in the middle of the night like some criminal. The school wasn't much help either. I will find you one day, and we'll live out those dreams we talked about and that's a promise I'll never break.

YOU'RE SCARING ME: FEMALE TEENAGER

I'd kind of been friends...well...known Callum, Cal, for a while. I remember we met when my brother was having a party. He was a couple of years older than me and we got on ok. We'd have a laugh together, but we only really saw each other because he was my brother's mate. He used to stay over at ours sometimes and he'd knock on my bedroom door and have a chat with me. He didn't stay long because my brother would always call for him. I think Nathan got a bit jealous he was paying me attention when he was supposed to be there to see him. I sometimes thought he was flirting, but I didn't fancy him and didn't see him like that. He was just a friend, a friend of my brothers. Kayla had been invited to an eighteenth at the local social club, she asked me to go with her. It was a friend of a guy who she'd met at the park. I said yes even though we didn't really know anyone that well. We thought it'd be a laugh and we'd probably be able to have a drink. We thought we'd pass for eighteen. I didn't tell my mum we were going to an eighteenth; I just said I was stopping over at Kayla's. We spent all afternoon choosing what we'd wear and listening to music. We arrived and it was pretty quiet but some guy offered us a drink and so we weren't going anywhere. It started to get busier and we were messing around on the dance floor. We'd had a few drinks by now and we couldn't really handle it. Kayla was spinning me around by my arm like we were on *Strictly Come Dancing* when I felt someone rub between my legs under my skirt. I turned around and it was Cal. I felt shocked and vulnerable, like he'd taken advantage, but I told myself it was probably an accident. He was a nice guy. Turns out he'd been at school with the lad whose birthday it was. I asked him where Nathan was. He said he might be calling in later. He didn't seem to want to talk about him and offered to buy me a drink. I said yes, of course, and Kayla was really jealous. She was stuck with a guy who'd fallen out of the ugly tree. Cal bought me a drink and went over to his mates. I could see them looking over at me and Kayla, but I couldn't hear what they were saying. Kayla said how fit Cal was. I felt flattered that he seemed to like me. Kayla kept telling me how he really fancied me. I told her it's just the way he was, a flirt. To me he was just my brother's mate. I just didn't fancy him. The night went on and Kayla and me were pretty wasted. We needed to get back to Kayla's when we realised we'd lost our bag. We'd put both our purses in it, and it was gone. We had no money for a taxi, and it was freezing, pouring down, we'd got no coats, our feet were killing and besides all that we could hardly put one foot in front of the other. Then Cal came over to us from nowhere. Like a guardian angel, we joked. He said he was going back to mine and we could get a lift. We thought he'd been sent from heaven in our drunken state. Nathan let us all in. Cal had already called him. Kayla went and sat in the front room with Rolo, Baggy, Cal and Nathan. I just needed to go to bed. I stumbled up the stairs and collapsed on my bed fully clothed. It felt amazing. I was asleep, when I felt that hand under my skirt again. My instinct was to freeze and tense my body. I knew, even though I still felt drunk, it was Cal. I could smell him. I started to roll over, I was trying to pull his hands off, but he just kept on touching me. His hands were pulling at my clothes, trying to undress me, inside my bra, under my skirt. I kept saying *you're scaring me, you're scaring me*. He started to undo his trousers and still I kept saying *you're scaring me, you're scaring me*. As I pulled his arms away and rolled away, mouthing *you're scaring me*, tears rolling down my cheeks, I looked straight into his eyes and he finally stopped fighting me. He just let go of me and rolled over. He fastened his trousers and lay silently next to me. I could still feel the heat from his body, but I just lay there too. Scared, frightened of what was next. After about five minutes of both lying motionless, he got up, said night to me and left. I heard him walk down the landing to my brother's room. When I woke up in the morning Kayla was in the bed next to me and last night felt like a bad dream. I knew it was real though. I could still smell Callum on my clothes. A button was ripped off my skirt and I could still feel his hands on my skin. I lay, remembering it, cringing, when Kayla rolled over and looked at me. She said she felt sick but she's had a wicked night. I said nothing.

I NEARLY DIED: FEMALE TEENAGER

I've always loved chewing gum. I've never really got why teachers have such a problem with it. Mrs Battersby says it's dangerous and if you swallow it, it blocks up your bowels. So, I googled it and she's wrong. I never trust a PE teacher when it comes to really intelligent things. She might be able to catch a ball and swim the English Channel but she's no Einstein. Anyway, Google said the human body cannot digest the gum base, but swallowed gum does not stay in the stomach or cause intestinal problems. The reason I first got into chewing gum was for my health, after all. I saw an article that said that people who chewed gum consumed sixty-eight fewer calories at lunch – that's like the calories in three whole chewy blue raspberry bon bons, or almost half a ripple bar, or even a quarter of a Big Mac, or somewhere about that. It also helps satisfy your cravings and resist fattening treats and stops your breath from smelling like Mr Bibby's death breath. Eugghhh. You'd think the teachers would be well impressed. I mean, I'm taking care of my personal hygiene and making an effort to eat fewer calories. It's like, they're always banging on about healthy eating and making the right choices. I was quite sure eating chewing gum was the right choice for me. I say was because I nearly died before. We were doing speeches in English and I was stood at the front of the room speaking and I opened my mouth to say piñata and somehow my chewing gum projected itself out of my mouth and straight into Alicia Brown's hair. Quite an impressive distance really but OMG she's like the most popular girl in the room and I'd just spat my spearmint fatty into her perfect hairdo. It flew from my open mouth so fast I almost thought no one might have noticed but the look on Alicia's face told me otherwise. Oh no, oh no. This was a very bad situation. I just wanted the earth to open up. The whole class gasped and tittered. Miss Amin stood up and slowly started walking towards Alicia's head. I think she was in as much confusion as me. How do we handle this? But then Alicia started to scream, get it off me, get it off me. It's like, I've not got foot and mouth disease or anything, but I sprang into action and quickly intercepted Miss Amin's approach and grabbed my piece of gum from Alicia's head – phew – but then I only went and popped it in my mouth. In my mouth! What was I thinking? Well, I just wasn't, and as I chewed it I could feel one of Alicia Brown's hairs tangling around my tongue. Everyone in the room started making gagging noises and shouting *eugghhh* and I got it because I was revolted in myself. I was gagging too. I bolted for the door, ran to the toilet, spat the stupid chewing gum in the bin and picked Alicia Brown's hair from between my teeth and, well, oh my days, I could have died. I mean, could it get any worse? So now I'm stuck here, and I don't know what to do. What do you reckon? Do I go back to class or never come back to school again?

A KICK AND A PUNCH: FEMALE TEENAGER

Skank, Chav. The daily routine of name-calling and torture starts again and it's not even nine o'clock. Another school day. Another day in hell. From the moment I arrive they're waiting. It's like they've got me under surveillance. Stalking their prey. The teachers don't seem to mind. After all, it's just playground banter, play fighting, nobody is getting seriously hurt. It's only a bit of fun, are you sure you didn't do something to provoke it? Everybody else seems to get on with them. Are you just feeling sorry for yourself? You need to show them who's boss, just ignore them, don't encourage it. I've heard the lot. It's not even worth mentioning any more. There's no help, no one cares and I'm just being a pathetic troublemaker. Uh, and then the bell, time for morning registration and just like every morning they shove me out of the way, push past me and start jabbing me in the neck with a ruler, all in good humour of course, just a bit of fun. Miss Browning doesn't even look up from the register. 'Settle down class' is her only comment as everyone laughs and titters at my expense. I'm just being silly getting upset though. I have to take it with a pinch of salt. Miss Browning's own wise words, the last time I mentioned it all to her. The bell rings, great, I've got to leave class and be at the mercy of their amusement as we walk down the corridor. It could be anything from a kick and a punch, a slap, jumping out behind me, taking my shoes, or even stealing my lunch money. It's just a bit of fun though, nothing serious. I don't know how I cope with all this fun in my life. Every day's just one big joke. I leave the classroom and there's not an ounce of suspense today, oh no, there it is, that voice, like nails on a blackboard, an awful screaming nightmare, the one and only Ellen Washington. 'Where's your lunch money? Check in her bag,' she says. I nervously reply, 'I left late this morning and forgot to pick it up. My mum's dropping it off later.' Ellen's having none of it. 'Search her,' she says in her demonic voice. Her minions grab at me and delve into my pockets and personal space. They only find my Mars bar. 'We'll have this for now, but by lunch you'll owe double,' they say. A final friendly kick and a punch and as quick as they appeared, the fun loving, excitable, little darlings disappear. I brush myself down, straighten my tie and practically skip down the corridor. I mean, that was so much fun, we were having such a laugh. Yeah right, Miss Browning, if that's your idea of having a laugh it explains why no one wants to marry you. I really don't want to be here. I hate my life so much.

WHAT'S MY TRIGGER?: FEMALE TEENAGER

I'm going to work later. It's only my second shift, waiting tables at the local restaurant. I just wanted some money...money I didn't have to ask Dad for and explain what I wanted to buy with it. He's quite over-protective these days and I just wanted to feel a bit of independence. It's not easy though, even just getting my uniform out. It stresses me just looking at it. I didn't think about it when I went for the interview. I was just thinking about getting the job. It's only a short-sleeved shirt but to me it's a big thing. I've spent years hiding my arms, my legs, covering up so no one would notice, and now I can't. Well, I could. I could keep hiding but not forever. I've got to start dealing with things. I tried to tell myself no one would notice but I could see they had. Last week was my first shift and I was already self-conscious, but I could see people looking and then I heard the whispers. They thought they were whispering but I heard the little girl say, 'That girl's got funny patterns on her arms,' and the mum, or whoever she was, just shushed her up and looked embarrassed. I don't know if that's worse than if she'd told her how they'd got there or how she presumed they'd got there, although it's pretty obvious. I'm a self-harmer. Well, I like to say *I was*. It's taboo like all scars, all deformities, we avoid discussing it, change the subject, pretend we haven't noticed, but I see the looks, the glances. I hear the whispers. I wanted to say something, to tell the little girl why, to explain how it'd seemed to help, to say how every scar's a painful memory, to tell her I was only her age when it started. To even explain the shame and guilt I felt and still feel. It started years ago. I don't really want to go into why, it was just a really upsetting time for me and I just didn't know how to cope. Cutting myself just became obvious somehow. It just seemed to be the answer. I don't even know where the idea came from, but it seemed to help with my feelings, the anger, the self-doubt, self-hatred, the hopelessness and the guilt. It was a distraction. I didn't know how to tell anyone how I felt. I didn't know who to tell how I felt. I didn't think my dad would understand. He was a mess himself. I didn't know how to say what I needed. I wasn't even sure what it was I wanted to say. I just needed to let the pain inside me out. It was a real physical pain inside my body that I just couldn't deal with and this somehow made it go away.

My dad found out eventually, but by then I'd got the scars. It got too hard to hide them. He was devastated, blamed himself, and couldn't understand why I'd even do that. I was sent for counselling. It helped in the end. At first it just felt like I was wasting my time, but it started to make sense. It wasn't easy, although it was good to feel like someone understood, someone was listening. I kept a diary to help understand my triggers. I'd sit on my hands so I couldn't do anything until the urges passed. It wasn't quick, it wasn't immediate, but I'm here now and I'm brave enough to let people see my scars. You see, for me it's a huge step, being able to put that short-sleeved shirt on and walk out that door.

MUM GOT POORLY: FEMALE TEENAGER

It's home time. Everyone's rushing off, jumping into their parent's cars and running for the school bus. Me, I wish the school day would last forever. Not that I'm a nerd or a geek or all the other names people who like school are called, no, because I know what's waiting for me when I get home – and I dread it. Home life wasn't always like this, in fact I used to look forward to going home. We were once a happy family, going for days out, enjoying barbecues, having our friends stay over. But it all changed when Mum got poorly. I ask myself how? And why? But I don't have any answers. Dad just couldn't face it and began to drink. He'd spend nights in the pub and he'd only come home because they'd kicked him out for being abusive and fighting. Mum was admitted to hospital and it seems like she's been gone forever. Dad, well he got made redundant from work. I think it was that or they'd have to sack him. He'd been in the job that long and they knew about Mum's illness, so they made allowances for him. So that was that. He could spend all day, every day in the pub. I had to look after my two younger brothers, cook, clean, bath them and make sure they went to school. We managed, well, I managed, but I so missed Mum. I just wanted her to tell me it'd be ok and that we'd all get back to normal. Our normal before she got poorly. The worst was yet to come though. It was eleven thirty at night and Dad came home so drunk he could hardly stand up, let alone dance, so why he put the music on so loud is a mystery. The whole house was woken up. Dad was happy for once, singing and dancing. The neighbours didn't see it like that, and next door were hammering on the wall for him to be quiet. The police arrived and they were really nice as they knew Dad and knew what we were going through, but Dad took it too far and he hit the policewoman. I could hear the neighbours, 'no wonder Chrissy's sick, with that to put up with.' Chrissy was...is...my mother and no, Dad never hit Mum. The reason for her mental health issues are unknown, but I suppose that's why she's still in hospital trying to get better. Dad, well, they had to arrest him even though they didn't want to. An ex-policeman arrested for being drunk and disorderly. Me, I don't want to go home. I know what's waiting for me and my brothers...the nice lady from social services and foster care.

PRANKED AGAIN: FEMALE TEENAGER

Right, who has my shoes and my socks? Oh, come on, it might be funny the first time, but every week? Really, is it really that funny? Ok, coming or not, to find where you illiterate morons have put my shoes this time. Oh, clever, yes it takes a real genius to find them there in the bin, covered in, what is that? Oh my god, it stinks. The dumb idiots have poured something onto and into my shoes in the bin. Yes, very funny. Oh, this is disgusting. Right, think. I know, I'll take the bin over to the shower and rinse the whole lot. I need to be careful not to get my uniform wet. Ok, well everyone's left for lunch and so I'll put my PE gear on and take a shower with my shoes. Right, here goes, yes that seems to be working, I'll be in the canteen for lunch earlier than usual. What the...? I don't believe it, I'm covered in what appears to be blue ink or dye. Ah, so you think you're really funny this time, don't you? Yes, because it's normal to put dye in the shower head. Sorry, Miss, what am I doing taking a shower in my lunch break? Why is the bin in the shower? Why on earth am I and all the shower area full of blue dye? If I told her, she wouldn't understand. It's the initiation of the Secret Bluebell Society. So, I said nothing.

GETTING EXPLOITED: FEMALE TEENAGER

Her name – let me see – I'm hesitating because, well, I really shouldn't say, it's sort of confidential. I tell you what, let's just call her Lisa for now. I mean, her real name may come out later, but I really don't think it's my place to tell you. Right, well, for now Lisa was obviously a girl, in fact a very unattractive girl, not my words but Miss Carver's. I know that sounds really cruel but that's what I heard her say to Mr Drake. They were both waiting for Lisa's parents to arrive to start the meeting with social services and I don't think they knew I was there, but I'd been sent to the facilities cupboard to find a mop. Anyway, that doesn't matter, let me tell you about Lisa. Look, I tell you what, I'll start from the beginning as I think that'll be easier. We all used to hang out together, there was about six or seven of us and we'd hang around the park, street corners or, if we were lucky, in someone's house. Lisa was always out with us but most of the time it was like she wasn't there. Does that make any sense? She was the quiet one of the group. She didn't seem to want to join in the conversations about boys and what we'd done at the youth centre. If I'm really honest I'm not sure why she hung around with us. She always seemed to look down her nose at everything we did. Like when Ella was telling us about sleeping with Mark Jacobs and Lisa was utterly disgusted. Anyway, we moved up a year and Lisa stopped hanging around with us, just like that. No explanation, she just avoided us. We weren't bothered as she was so quiet, we didn't really miss her. She began to skip classes and when she was there, she seemed preoccupied, you know, her mind was elsewhere. Donna asked if she had a boyfriend or a girlfriend, but she just walked off. I mean you have to ask these things, don't you? There was just no talking to her. She started being really moody and even lost it with one of our teachers. Honestly, I'd never seen anything like it. Well, we didn't know how to help her or if we could even help her, she just seemed to go a bit mad. Donna said *leave the weirdo she's a head case*, not really helpful but who were we to get involved, and you don't go against Donna's wishes as well, she really was a head case and so were all her family. Put it this way, most of Donna's family were regular guests of the Queen. That's what my dad says and by that he means they've been in prison. Anyway, back to Lisa. This one night she turns up at mine out of the blue. No *sorry I've not seen you for ages*, but she wanted to talk and...well...I love a bit of gossip. So, we sat chatting and she tells me everything that's been going on. It turns out she'd been seeing this guy she met on the internet. I don't think they'd met up, it was like a cyber affair. Well he started asking her to send pictures of herself and I'm thinking, *well, she's not the most attractive*. Miss Carver's words, not mine. Anyway, it turns out it wasn't her face he wanted photos of but her fanny. Well, I was utterly gobsmacked and even more so when she told me she'd sent him some. Why would you even do that? I mean, she'd never met the guy. She'd only spoken to him online, but listen, it gets even creepier. Now that he had photos he was threatening her that if she didn't sleep with him, you know, have sex, he'd only go and post the pictures of her fanny online for the whole school and her family to see. I asked her what she was going to do, and she said that she'd have to sleep with him. I was in a right dilemma. Do I keep her secret and she gets even further involved or do I tell? Well, I didn't sleep all weekend and then I thought *she's in trouble and I know she can be a real pain but she's our friend, or she was*. Anyway, I grassed and I'm not proud of myself, because one thing everyone hates around our way is a grass. But I know I did the right thing. I stopped Lisa getting exploited even further, Miss Carver's words not mine. Well, I hope I have.

MAN UP: MALE TEENAGER

The outside image of me just doesn't fit with my personality. I've ne been a boy's boy. Ever since I was little my family would say, *man up, don't be such a girl.* I've tried all my life to man up and it's not working. I always have to remind myself to be manlier but I'm just not that good an actor. I can't keep it up twenty-four hours a day. It's exhausting. I've always had hang ups about my body but over the last year I've come to the conclusion I'm a girl in a boy's body. I'm scared to death of the thought of being transgender. I don't want that label. I'm only seventeen and I'm trying to get a job and fit in. I just want to be normal. I just want to make something of myself and live happily ever after. I really don't want to be some weird freak with a label, but I can't deal with these feelings anymore. I can't make them go away. I've joined an LGBT group near me, and I've been going for a few months. They've all been really supportive and they're all so brave. They've helped me understand my feelings. A lot of them have had really positive experiences coming out, telling their parents. Being accepted by loved ones has made it so much easier for them to accept themselves. In the end that's what gave me the courage to tell my parents. It didn't go brilliantly but it wasn't terrible. They didn't throw me out and tell me never to darken their door again, like in the scenario I'd been replaying over and over in my mind since the moment I decided to tell them. Mum and Dad said they still love me, but they blame 'that stupid group' I joined for filling my head with mumbo jumbo. 'It's just a phase,' they said walking out of the room. I never mentioned it again and it was as if the problem had gone away. They were happy to just ignore it and just pretend like the conversation never happened, leaving me trying to be the son they want. I knew I couldn't pretend forever though. Ever since I realised I was a girl trapped in a boy's body, I still can't call myself transgender, and I can't stop thinking about being a woman. I see girls and start to imagine what their life must be like. I'm so envious and I really hate the body I've been given. I often get the urge to harm my body, to hack it away from my personality, to tear it off and expose the real me. I was so scared of the thought of the procedure to have a sex change but I'm even more scared about being rejected by my family and friends. I just felt stuck inside this carcass with no escape without the help of the ones I love. I had to keep questioning *do I live for them or do I live for me*. I didn't expect it; it was a total surprise, a real shock. Totally out of the blue Mum says she's got an appointment at a gender identity clinic. 'For me or for you,' I say confused. 'For you of course,' she replies with a smile. I couldn't hide my tears. They were listening, they just needed time. I smiled, I cried, and we hugged.

SILENT TALK: FE/ MALE TEENAGER

A car, a car, there's someone parking up. Quiet, sshhh, quiet, it's Alfie, he's back, he's coming in. He'll hear you. He'll know we're here. Who thought this was a good idea anyway? I thought you said he was away for the weekend with his – oi Nobby, shut it. Did you hear that? He's in the door. He's coming up the stairs. What we gonna do? Shit, what we gonna do? Stay calm, stay calm. My dad'll kill me. He will know we're here if you don't all shut it. Ssshh, he's outside the door. Oh shit, oh shit. Ah phew, he's going back downstairs. Sshh! He's talking to someone – must be his new – hold on, that's my mum's voice. What's my mum doing in the pub at this time with Alfie. Woah, oh no, no, no, no. Tell me she's not having it off with him. Tell me I'm wrong. This can't be happening. Shut up, shut up, you want me to shut up, when my mum's about to get it– *(Alfie enters)*. Oh, hello Alfie. What am I doing here? What are you doing here with my mum?

ATTENTION-SEEKING FEMALE: FEMALE TEENAGER

It's always the same and I'm fed up with hearing it. My mum and dad are so prehistoric but to be honest, most of society still are. Can I ask what did women fight for? Why on earth did Emily Davidson throw herself in front of a horse? What does the Suffragette movement mean to women of today? We've come such a long way but still not far enough. Mum always makes me help with the washing up. I ask her, 'why don't you ask Dad or my brothers to help? They've eaten off the plates, drunk out of the glasses and used the knives and forks.' She glares at me and says, 'its not a man's job.' What? And why not? Tell me, Mum, why do women have to clean the house? Dad and my brothers live here as well. Why do women do all the washing and ironing? Do men not wear clothes? Why is it that none of the males in our house cook? Do they not eat the food? Oh, wait, but when BBQ season starts males are the only ones who can cook outdoors, shouting for plates, the food, cooking utensils, oh and not forgetting another beer. Why is it expected that women stay at home and look after the children? Why should women put their careers on hold or give them up entirely? Are the males not the fathers? Shouldn't it be their turn to take control of the family and share the responsibility? Take Christmas, we all open our presents and then the men go to the pub whilst the women cook. What's that all about? Whoever said that men are the stronger sex must have been having a laugh. Yes, physically most might be stronger, but in my opinion females are far more superior in knowledge, perseverance and multi-tasking. However, don't tell my mum or else I'll be shouted at again and told I'm attention-seeking and trying to get out of my chores. So, this attention-seeking female will bite her lip until the day comes when she meets a househusband, or at least a man who'll share the housework.

THERE'S SOMETHING I NEED TO TELL YOU: MALE TEENAGER

I've got something to tell you. Erm...I need to let you know. I've been meaning to say. I think there's something you should know. I'm erm... I erm...the thing is...how do you tell someone something you know they don't want to hear? Someone that really means something to you. How do you break something to them that you know they don't want to hear? You think about it loads. I am. Then you try to plan out the conversation. Your move. Their move. Do alternative scenarios. But they always end the same way. With them getting upset. That's something I don't want. I've spent my whole life trying to make them proud. That's what all kids really want isn't it. For their parents to be proud of them, and then I got this thrown at me. I can't help it. I can't change it. It's who I am. It's how I feel. I probably wouldn't choose it because I'm not what you wanted me to be. I'm never going to be a perfect son. I mean, I always wanted to wear girl's clothes. As I've got older it's got harder. I mean, there's a turning point where it's not cute and laughable anymore. That point where it becomes serious and a problem. I think this is going to be that really big moment where I have to admit it. We'll all have to face up to the problem. I can't avoid the conversation for much longer. I'm sat in a police car being driven home from town. I'm not old enough to be wandering the streets in a dress past midnight. It seemed a good idea these last couple of months. It kind of made me feel real. Now I just feel stupid. My mum and dad never knew. I snuck out when everyone was in bed. It was the best time, when hardly anyone was about. But now they'll know. The car's indicating to turn down our street. We're pulling up at my front door. I'm anxious, I'm clammy. How can I get out of this? I'll be alright here, thanks. No really, you don't have to see me in. Oh, ok. I've literally got moments to decide how I tell them. Do I need to say anything? I'm stood here in a dress. The hall light's turning on. I can't bear it. I can hear the key turning in the lock. What do I say? Hi, there's something I need to tell you...

I MISS YOU DAD: FEMALE TEENAGER

It's been over a year since it happened. I remember it like it was yesterday. I was at home in my room texting Bex, making plans to meet up, when Mum came in. She sat me down and told me the news. 'It's Dad,'she said softly, with a look in her eyes like I'd never seen before. 'He's got cancer.' I instantly felt panic, grief even. I seemed to sink into the bed and a thousand questions raced around my head, but all the words wouldn't come out. What was going to happen to him? Was he going to die? I was shocked. I couldn't take it in. I saw him this morning, there was nothing wrong with him. How can he have cancer? I'd slammed the door in his face for telling me I couldn't see Liam. I muttered *I hate you* under my breath as I stormed up the stairs. I didn't mean it though. I didn't want this to happen. I didn't want him to die. He was my dad, and everything a dad should be. Mum kept talking, it's spread to his lymph nodes. I wasn't taking it in. I could only hear words, not sentences. Clavicle, lungs, kidney. It didn't make sense. How could it? He was fine. I didn't cry, I couldn't. She must be wrong. 'He'll be ok,'she said hugging me. 'Remember, he's a fighter.' She lied. He wouldn't be alright, he wouldn't get better and he'd just change from my big, strong hero to a weak shell of himself. She lied. Why my dad? Why me? Why couldn't they save him? Why? Why? Why? The cancer took everything, until there was no more to take, until he was gone. I wish...I wish...I could see him...in the kitchen eating breakfast. I wish he'd tell me I couldn't see Liam, so I could slam the door in his face again. I wouldn't mutter that I hated him under my breath though. I'd never say that again. He was right about Liam. It didn't last. I miss you Dad. I love you so much.

PLAYER ONE: FE/MALE TEENAGER

They look at me and they just see a fool. I'm different, I get that. I feel it every day. Every minute. I'm uncomfortable with life. I'm uncomfortable with people. I can see them looking at me. Wanting me to look back and meet their stare. Make eye contact. They've always told me to make eye contact. It makes me twitch, it makes me nervous, I don't know when to start and then I don't know when to stop. How long is too long? How long should I look into their eyes? I don't know. One second seems like forever. I'm shifty, freaky, weird, geeky. I'm stand offish, cold, unaffectionate, alone. I just wanted to teach them not to think I'm stupid. I'm many things, I'm all the things they call me but I'm not stupid. Don't underestimate that. Well, I've played the game and I've beat them so now I can depart, leave this platform, sign out, log out and not look back. I've nothing else to prove. I've made my point. That's my game over. That's my game done. I'm leaving a winner. Player one, number one. Done. When you're gone, you're gone.

I T'S ALL ABOUT THE GIRL: MALE TEENAGER

It's always all about the girl, it's always her choice, but I wanted a choice – I wanted a say. It wasn't just up to her, but at the same time it was her body. I couldn't do much about it. She'd have to carry it, she'd have to give birth, but that baby growing inside her was mine too. Mine, and I loved it. I know we were too young. I know we were only kids. I know we'd be changing our futures...but...I wanted to give it a life, to love it. I told her I'd be a good dad. She looked at me and scoffed, *what? Even though you're still at school. How can we look after a baby?* But it won't be forever, just another year and I'll get a job, my mum and dad will help us. Please don't do this. But I didn't have a say. I couldn't stop her going through with it. It was her choice, not mine. It wasn't just a fling, I really loved her, I wanted us to be a family, but instead I had to go with her. I had to sit in the clinic. Sit whilst they looked at us like we were immature kids taking the easy option. This wasn't the easy option for me. I wish we'd listened to everyone nagging us, telling us to be careful, but we were just kids having a good time, we weren't worrying about consequences, we were just having fun. It doesn't feel like fun anymore. My baby will never get to have fun. I watched it on the monitor. It was alive and its heart was beating. Today its heart doesn't beat anymore. It felt like I'd taken a gun to my own child. It broke me. But I had no choice. It's not about the boy; it's all about the girl. We didn't last after that. I blamed her and she blamed me. She should have gone on the pill. But now I see I had a choice. I should have used a condom. I should have taken responsibility. I shouldn't have left it all up to her. I always thought it would be her problem if she got pregnant but it turned out it was mine too.

IT WAS ALL ABOUT HIM: FEMALE TEENAGER

He made out it was all my fault. It happened because I didn't take the pill, because I wasn't careful. Like I wanted to end up pregnant. I didn't want a baby. I couldn't even do my own washing. I didn't know how to cook an egg and there I was up the duff at sixteen. He wanted to keep it. Well, it wasn't his body that'd have it growing inside him, stretching it out and messing it up. I didn't feel ready for a baby. But it was all about him. My feelings didn't matter. I was taking his baby away. I wasn't giving him a choice. I didn't know how he felt. I was being immature. I was being selfish. I just wanted some support. It was the worst time. I thought we'd made the right choice. He disagreed. He thought I'd taken the easy option. It didn't feel like an easy option to me. I wish we'd listened to everyone nagging us, telling us to be careful, but we were just kids having a good time, we weren't worrying about consequences, we were just having fun. It doesn't feel like fun anymore. My baby will never get to have fun. I watched it on the monitor, it was alive and its heart was beating. Today its heart doesn't beat anymore. It felt like I'd taken a gun to my own child. It broke me. But I had no choice. It's not just about him. We didn't last after that. I blamed him and he blamed me. He should have used a condom. But now I see I had a choice. I should have gone on the pill. I should have taken responsibility. I shouldn't have left it all up to him. I always thought it wouldn't happen to me.

RADICALISATION: MALE TEENAGER

I don't have much in common with most of the kids around here. I do well at school, but I'd say I'm too intelligent for them all really. I just keep my head down and don't draw attention to myself. The thing is, this is my country, these are my people, but I don't feel like I belong here. Do you know what I mean? I don't feel like people understand my opinions, my views. I got involved last year, there was a guy in town reciting stuff. There were a lot of haters telling him to leave, shouting at him. That's what got my interest. He was really passionate and everything he said just seemed to make sense. Have you heard him? Tall guy with a really deep powerful voice. I took a flyer off him and went to a meeting. Everyone there seemed to be feeling the same as me. Like they know we're losing control too. They made me feel welcome. Even though I was one of the youngest there they treated me with respect and made me feel like my opinions mattered. I didn't take it too seriously at the time. It was just about belonging. Then I started to get bullied by this gang. They called themselves the Hanky Park Lot. They laughed at me, ridiculed me, and made me feel worthless. They made me angry. They made me see everything that was wrong with this society. No one was there to listen. No one cared. My parents were too busy trying to get by. This society has just forgotten me. They don't care about people like me. We have to start fighting for our rights, fighting for more for ourselves. Now I've got the incentive and I've got the opportunity. I've only been to a few demonstrations and just being able to shout and march like an army, an army with a strong voice, a voice people are scared of, to be part of that makes me feel like I can take on the world. I'm not on anyone's radar. I'm just a kid, just a normal kid. We'll show them. I haven't told my parents. They don't take an interest in much of what I do. How about you? What are your thoughts? Look, I know I'm getting deeply involved in this. I know a lot of people wouldn't agree with what I'm doing, but the way I see it we have to make our voice heard. So here we are, it's good to finally meet you. I've been organising stuff for the attack like you said. I haven't discussed it with anyone else and I took note – I haven't used my own computer for anything, and I got a new pay-as-you-go sim. I've got a contact that can get me a gun if needed though. No, no, don't worry, I didn't tell him the plans, didn't mention anything about anything. Said it was for my older brother's friend who wants to put the frighteners on someone and I encrypted the files on how to make the pressure cooker backpack bomb with a switch detonator when I put them on my computer. I got hold of another, 'how to make a bomb from your mom's kitchen' but it didn't sound as powerful. I've managed to get some of the gear. I've been grinding up matchstick heads relentlessly. See this powder, looks like nothing, boom, it'll ignite. Is the plan still to leave it at a busy point? Just leave it and go. We'll just stand back and watch the chaos. All of them running and screaming, getting what's coming. Sorry, hold on. What? No, no, I'm fine. Right, I'll come down in a minute. No, he's fine too, he's leaving soon. Sorry, my mum wanting to know if you want food. Yeah, so I think you're right, after prayers just as everyone's leaving. Did you manage to check out any locations? I looked at a couple. Lot of CCTV in the centre. Do you not think somewhere on the outskirts might be better, there'd be a lot less chance of us being seen? Here look, this is the pressure cooker. Did you manage to get the pipes and caps? You're definitely still up for this? We're definitely going to do this? Shit, what's that banging, what the...shit...shit...it's the feds, open the window, throw it. Shit, we're being raided.

CLASS EDUCATION: FE/MALE TEENAGER

I think some things are more important than education. I hear you teachers shouting *don't be so disrespectful* but let me explain. I'm not saying it to be defiant like you think. I'm not saying it to be disrespectful like you tell me I am. I'm saying it because it's what I believe. We all have our beliefs. I mean some us believe in God, some of us believe in medicine, some people believe in war. I believe in weed. Nah, nah I'm joking. Some people have no sense of humour. I think we need beliefs. I think we need to believe in something. It gets you through life and I believe some things are more important than education. I mean, you can teach me to read, you can teach me to write, but what's more human than feeling? Feeling an emotion. You can't teach me that. You have to go out and do it, live it, see it, get it. You can show me a photo, but I can't smell it, I can't hear it, I don't truly feel it. You can read me a book, but unless you've been there do you truly feel it? Like, we're in class reading *Romeo and Juliet* and you tell me they love each other but I don't know what true love feels like, and you can't teach me that. I have to go out and find it. I feel real love for this person, and you didn't teach me that. I felt it. We made it happen, our relationship. We shared it. We worked at it. We built it, and you want me to end it like this. Without me being there for her when she needs me most. I think when I'm like thirty or something, this moment will be more important to me than any education you teach me here at school. So, the thing is, I need time off to go visit her. I asked Miss Wood for time off and she outright said no. Like I'd just asked her if I could go out to visit the corner shop. Swear down, she's got no feelings. Well, course I got a bit angry. I mean she doesn't like me anyway; she never has. I know I shouldn't have kicked off, but she just doesn't care. Maybe she needs some belief in something, belief in love. I don't think she feels anything. She didn't care at all. It's like control. She's got control over something really important to me. I only asked 'cos I thought it was the right thing to do. I should've just gone. It's none of her bloody business anyway. You see it's my gran. I just got a text from my mum. She's actually dying. She's dying and I feel real love for her. She's taught me loads. I want to go see her, feel her, touch her, speak to her, see her before she, you know, dies. I want to tell her I love her and look deep into her eyes, into her soul. It'll be her final lesson to me. I love my gran. I'm going to miss her more than anything. I don't know what I'll do without her. What will I do? Please, please let me go, Sir. I really believe I need to do this more than I need to read Shakespeare. I can read Shakespeare tomorrow. I can't hold her hand and tell her how much I love her tomorrow. Tomorrow she'll be gone.

XBOX REALITY: MALE TEENAGER

My life was gaming. Don't get me wrong, I wasn't like some sad computer geek with no social skills, I was actually quite popular. But after school I'd just spend all night on my Xbox. Escaping to fantasy worlds. I'd play with my mates and we'd chat but as the levels went up and I got better, I'd sometimes play against strangers. I'd always get to know and trust them first though. I'd learnt to be careful after Mum confiscated all my games consoles because I swore online. I had to explain why I wasn't gaming to my mates – it wasn't cool, and I felt a right tool. So now I thought about what I got up to and made sure my mum wasn't sniffing about. Anyway, I'd just finished eating and I went back upstairs to my room. I sat down on my Xbox and started playing COD. I'm playing Xbox live and this girl comes online and asks me to add her. I thought, well, where's the harm in that. A girl's not going to beat me – and I was right, I annihilated her. Then she said her older brother wanted his machine back. After a couple of hours of playing against him he left, and I started to get messages from his sister again. We chatted for about an hour and then I told her I had to go. The following evening, she was back online, and we went straight in to the chat room and completely forgot about the game. Even though I was popular I didn't have much confidence around girls but felt so much more at ease with her. Kylie was her name. We chatted for days by text, she said she didn't want her brother knowing all her business. Which I get. We were really getting on and then she sent me a photo of herself and she was gorgeous. She asked would I send a photograph of myself and I agreed, I mean what's the harm in that? She said she thought I was cute and a couple of days later she sent me a photo of herself without a top on and she'd got me hooked. I was fourteen years old and hormones were running riot. She asked for some of me, you know, without clothes on, and, well, I trusted her by now. It just seemed natural, not weird or anything. She eventually suggested that we meet, and I was definitely up for it. She said I could call to hers and meet her mum. It all seemed harmless. Although I knew my mum would've gone up the wall if I told her I was actually meeting up with someone I'd met online. So, I just told her I was going to town with my mates. Mum dropped me in town and asked where my friends were. I said they'd gone earlier to watch a film, but I wasn't interested. Mum kissed me goodbye and said she'd collect me later. I hated lying to Mum, but she really wouldn't understand. I reached the address of the girl and I knocked on the door. An old guy opened the door and said he was Kylie's dad and she'd just gone shopping with her mum and wouldn't be long. Once I entered the house, he locked the door. He said it was a rough neighbourhood. I felt a little uneasy. He then offered me a drink. The house didn't look very clean and I refused, after all I wasn't staying long. He sat down and told me he had all the photographs I'd sent Kylie. I couldn't believe it. She'd let her dad see them and I'd trusted her. He then said there was no Kylie. What? I didn't understand. And then it got worse. He said if I didn't agree to sleep with him, he'd share the photos of me online for all my family and friends to see. What was going on? Things like this don't happen to me, they happen on television to other people. What would my family say? What would my friends say? I'd be ridiculed and humiliated. I told him I couldn't do it. He got really aggressive and wrestled me over and pinned me down on the floor. What do I do now? I couldn't breathe. I was trapped with this man on top of me, who must've been in his fifties with his yellow nicotine-stained fingers wrapped tightly around my wrists, wanting me to perform some sort of sexual act with him. No one even knew I was here. Oh Jesus what was he about to do? How can I stop it all? He started unbuttoning his trousers and he began to rip off my top. I still couldn't get my breath. I froze and started to cry like a baby. What had I got myself into? I closed my eyes. The door flew open and police came running in. It was like some sort of computer game or a scene from a Hollywood movie. I was still crying. I was still crying and gasping like a little kid. They helped me up from the floor. Lucky for me the police had been watching him for a while. He was a well-known paedophile. I'd trusted a predator. What an idiot. How could I be so stupid? Well of course my parents had to find out but they don't like talking about it. Instead I go to a therapist. My friends don't understand why I don't do gaming anymore. I couldn't possibly tell them the truth. I'm so ashamed. I had a very lucky escape and I know it. I still have the nightmares to remind me.

I CAN'T BREATHE: MALE TEENAGER

I told myself, *come on do it for your future self,* but I'm stood here waiting and I don't even feel like my future self will be here. I think this may be the end of my future self. I'm not sure I'm going to make it. I'm scared, petrified, I don't even know how I ended up here. Peer pressure. I was pressured into this and I'm not sure I'm ready for it. You told me it'd be fun. I don't think it will be. You called me a wuss. You pushed me in. You called me a chicken. You didn't give me a choice. My heart's racing. What did that nurse say? Deep breath in, hold for three, breathe out and repeat. *(Act out breathing in and out.)* I'm moving closer and I'm not feeling any better. What's here? *(Holds hand to chest where heart is.)* What's here? My heart? I'm getting a pain. I don't think I can do this. Am I having a heart attack? No, my arms are fine. No, I don't feel dizzy. No, I'm not hot, clammy, tingling. I'm just scared to death. That saying means people must actually die from fear. Breathe Ben, breathe. *(Acts out breathing.)* I can see the headline: *Thirteen-year-old dies from fear following peer pressure to go on rollercoaster.* What an embarrassing way to die, but would it be more embarrassing not to actually get on the ride? I don't think I can do it. Will you hold my hand? No, I'm not gay. I'm scared. Move along where? Who? Me? You want me to move? You want me to stand at that barrier? Hold my hand. Don't take the mick mate, I'm really frightened. Just hold my hand. Don't be like that. Please...Please...it's not funny. I'm serious, help me out. I can't do it. Stop filming me. I can't breathe. Stop it. Stop it. I can't breathe.You're supposed to be my mate. Stop it. Stop It. I don't want to do it. I can't do it. I can't do it. I don't want to. Let me out...let me out of here. Stop filming me. Stop laughing. Stop filming me. I'm serious. Let me out. Let me out now. Let me out. Just let me out now.

ESCAPE REALITY: FEMALE TEENAGER

I sometimes imagine I'm Harry Potter. It helps me escape this world. I often take myself off on my broomstick, in my mind of course. It gives me a different perspective on things, especially when Mrs Brown is rambling on about the shift of tectonic plates. I'm climbing on my air powered zoom broom, taking to the ceiling, and just about to start my next mission. Firstly, I hover over my motley classmates picking today's target. Enemy in sight – The ever-orange Chelsea Boggins, the loud-mouthed, lardy, bully of the class. She's the leader of the Oompa Loompas orange brigade. She ridiculed me this morning for being a freak. I smirk to myself. I carefully load up a water bomb into the power jet, I zoom in on the target and adjust the sights. I press the blaze button and the balloon of water whizzes out and forcefully splats onto Chelsea Boggins' head. The colour drains from her cheeks leaving a well of what looks like tomato soup resting in her skirt. I'm satisfied my work here is done. Next, to move on to one of Chelsea's minions. I do a triumphant lap of the room before coming to a resting hover over Sinead Dodd. Her bright orange hair blending with her tangerine tan. She is the Ron Weasley of the class. I load up a ketchup cartridge into the splat gun and get ready to pull the trigger. I'm adjusting the sights, hovering silently over my target when I start to feel a piercing burn in my aura. My being is under scrutiny. I can sense eyes on me. I zoom out from my intrepid mission to splat and see Mrs Brown's eyes staring straight at me. I focus on her presence. She's stood hand on hip, pointing at the white board. I can't hear her yet. I'm not fully back in the room, but she is definitely mouthing a question in my direction. I re-establish myself back into the mundane world of reality. I can hear her now. Nicola Lancaster what is continental drift? That's my name. That question is aimed at me, but I have no idea what the answer is. Do I justify why I don't know the answer by sharing my mission to destroy the orange army? I think better of it. I don't know, Miss. Why don't I know? Erm...er...I just wasn't paying attention, Miss.

A BRUTAL LIE: FEMALE TEENAGER

I told a bit of a fib last year. Well, I didn't tell the truth, to be honest I told a brutal lie. I didn't mean for things to turn out the way they did, I just didn't want my mum and dad to know the truth, so I lied to them. No big deal, I'd done it a thousand times before, but this was serious. It wasn't just like *no I didn't eat the last packet of crisps or no I didn't spend my dinner money on makeup*. It would affect someone else's life...it would affect mine forever. I'll start from the beginning. I was at my friend's house and her older brother was there with his mates and they were having a bit of a party. He was in charge of the house whilst their mum and dad were on holiday. We weren't invited, we were just there. His mates were all really fit and seemed really mature compared to the boys in my year at school. We were just hanging around when Iggy started chatting to me. I was gobsmacked he was like the hottest boy in school, when he was there. He asked me how old I was and I told him I was sixteen, which was the first lie in the story because I was actually only fifteen, but I thought it sounded better being sixteen. He told me he was nineteen. I thought he was gorgeous. We carried on talking until we kissed, and it was amazing. He took my number and said he'd be in touch. I was so happy. The next day he messaged me, and I was so excited. Anyway, we met and it wasn't long before we had sex and it was amazing. That night I was at home when I got a message from Iggy, except I'd left my phone downstairs and my dad picked it up. It was only short - *Wen you goin to let me do that to you again?* My dad came banging on my door asking, *who is this from? What does he mean? What's he done to you? Does he know how old you are? How do you know him?* I started to panic. I started to tell him where we met, and he looked so angry so I started to lie. I started to lie to protect myself from the shame and embarrasment. I didn't want to tell my dad he was fit, we met the other day, we'd had great sex and I loved it. So, I told him we met at a party, he's nineteen, he said my age didn't matter, he took advantage of me when I was drunk. He took photos and keeps messaging me. It was all lies, but it made me look like the victim. It made me look like the person my dad thought I was. I thought that'd be it. I thought he'd just hug me and say it'll be alright, but he didn't.

He told me to put a coat on, we were going to the police. I didn't know what to say. I just did as he said and when the policewoman asked me what happened, I lied to her too. I couldn't stop. Before I knew it, they'd arrested Iggy. I didn't mean for any of it to happen. People were calling him a paedo, they wrote it across the front of his mum's house. They threw stuff out of cars as they drove past. Iggy told the truth about what happened, but no one believed him. He was charged with having sex with a minor. It was going to court. He wouldn't plead guilty. Why would he? I lied about my age. I'd have to go to the trial and testify but, well it never came to that. I can't bring myself to say what happened, but I can tell you this much. I would rather have just admitted we had slept together, that I really liked him, than have the responsibility of someone's death on my hands. It's with me as soon as I wake up. I can't get rid of my conscience and I'll always be the liar. I can never tell the truth.

IT'S JUST NOT COOL: MALE TEENAGER

It's hard being thirteen and three quarters. Older people think we've got it easy, but I don't know. I'm finding being a teenager pretty difficult. It's like, I'm not sure who I am, where I fit in. Am I a child or am I an adult? I mean, I like my mum fussing over me, doing everything for me, but then at times I need her to know she can't. The thing is I've just got a girlfriend. She's alright I think, although when my mum looked at a photo the first thing she said was *does she look better in real life*. I didn't know how to take that really. I mean, I don't want to be dating someone everyone else thinks is ugly. Like I say, I don't mind my mum fussing over me but just when we're on our own. It's like, the other day I finally took my girlfriend round to mine. We were sitting in my room chatting when Mum barges in and gives me a kiss saying, 'are you alright baby? Do you want fish fingers for your tea?' I mean, it's just not cool. How can I have a girlfriend when my mum calls me baby and seriously, only little kids eat fish fingers. I start to think whether she's done it on purpose because she thinks my girlfriend doesn't look better in real life, she looks a whole lot worse. Then I think, no, it's just Mum being Mum, embarrassing. Maybe I need to sit her down and just tell her I'm growing up, set her some ground rules. One, don't call me baby. Two, don't hug me or kiss me in public. Three, don't tell people I'm scared of the dark. Four, don't mention that I...Mum...Mum is that you? Will you just come in here a minute? Yeah, my room. Hi Mum. I just wanted to ask you something. Yeh, that was one thing, don't call me baby. Yeah, I am hungry actually. Erm...actually can I have fish fingers and chips. Yeah, with loads of ketchup.

NO ONE WILL LISTEN: FEMALE TEENAGER

Just because I'm young doesn't mean I don't have opinions. I'm always getting talked down to. That's how it feels anyway. Not heard out. I start saying the speech I've rehearsed over and over in my head out loud for their ears...and...they just cut me short. They interrupt me. 'Let me just stop you there, Ellie.' This is a big moment for me. I'm going to spill my soul, share my weaknesses. The sort of moment you never forget...and...they don't even let me finish the words I wanted to say, the words I had crafted, cried over, had sleepless nights reworking. To them I'm just another kid, just another face, another mark on a sheet, a criteria. Someone to deal with, an issue. What about my voice? What about my opinion? What about how I really feel? How I really think? How I really hurt? How no one hears me out? All that's left to do is shrug and nod. My voice is not heard. My words are not wise. My tears are that of crocodiles. My hands shaking are a nuisance, unnecessary, an act. They'll never understand why I really did it. They'll never understand what it's like to be me. Not because it's too hard to comprehend. Not because it's too horrific to make sense of. They'll never understand because no one will listen. No one wanted to listen then. That's how it all started in the first place. I'll play it over in my mind. I'll repeat my speech to myself. In the background I can still hear them but now I don't want to listen. I start my speech in my head – *I felt the weight on top of me, I tried to push, but I couldn't move. I couldn't stand up. I was fighting, it was hurting, and I shouted stop, but it didn't. I moved my arms and I got hold of the first thing I found, and I swung it as fast as I...*'Ellie, are you listening to us?' 'Piss off,' I shout as I wave my arms with force and freedom. They interrupted me again. It was the wrong time to interrupt me. I hate you all. They grab me and so it starts again. 'How can we believe your side of the story if this is how you react when we try and talk to you?' And again. 'How can we trust you to tell the truth when all you do is shout and swear?' I go weak, drop my head. I weep inside. They don't talk to me, they talk at me, they talk over me. I don't want them to talk to me. I just want someone to listen.

RUN FOR MY LIFE: MALE TEENAGER

'Booms' to be shouted like someone shouting Boo and making you jump.

Boom. I feel a hand touch my shoulder. Boom. My heart jumps. Boom. I jump. I didn't hear them coming. I didn't see their shadows approaching. I was alone with my music. Looking forward to seeing my girlfriend. Walking down a street I'd walked down a thousand times before. Boom. I jump forward. Boom. I turn to look. A silver blade glides through the fabric of my coat glistening in the moonlight. Boom. My heart beats faster. They're gesturing at me. It's all moving in slow motion. The music's still playing in my ears. Through the tunnel. Boom. They rip my headphones off and suddenly it seems almost silent as my ears adjust to the shock and then the muffled threats, shouts, taunts, rise from under their disguises. Turn out your pockets. What's in your pockets? Where's your phone? Where's your phone? They grab at me. They keep shouting. I'm overcome with panic. Boom. I throw my phone. Boom. They scurry towards it like wild animals on a kill. I can see the blade catching the light in the dark. Boom. I turn. Boom. I run. I run like my life depends on it – it might do. I can hear their footsteps behind me. Thudding, thumping, beating, drumming; constantly drumming towards me. Thudding, thumping, beating, drumming. Thudding, thumping, beating, drumming. Thudding, thumping, beating, drumming. I daren't look back. I daren't turn around. Their jeers fade. Their threats lower. I catch their last taunt as I turn the corner. Next time it'll be more than your coat, do you hear me? I keep running. I keep running until I reach the door. I hammer hard and fast. The light comes on in the hall. The relief to see a familiar face. The relief to hear a loving voice. The relief to have made it. I've never been so scared. I've never felt such panic. I've never run for my life before.

PERSONAL STRUGGLES: FEMALE TEENAGER

I've always looked at Frankie Shepherd and thought she's everything I want to be. She's beautiful, she's popular, intelligent, funny, thin, confident. I've always wished I could be her. I'm everything she isn't. I'm ugly, lonely, stupid, fat and anxious. I can't tell you the amount of time I've spent watching everything she does and trying to copy it. The way she lets her coat hang off her shoulder. The way she laughs. The way she flicks her hair. The way she walks. I can't remember the amount of times I've thought to myself *I wish I was Frankie Shepherd; she's got the most perfect life*. You can imagine how shocked I was when Kelly told me. She told me Frankie had got MS, Multiple Sclerosis. I mean, I wasn't sure what that meant but it sounded serious and we looked it up. It is serious. It makes sense now because she had been having a lot of time off school but how could someone so perfect be so ill? I couldn't believe I'd been sat wishing to be her whilst all along she'd been secretly suffering. I mean it made me feel a little luckier to be me and even stupider. Frankie still looks as great as ever and you'd never have guessed there was anything wrong really, because she always put on a brave face. Then I noticed her friends weren't bothering with her as much. Some people even started calling her a liar because she could walk. That's when I started talking to her and she felt just as ugly, lonely, stupid, fat and anxious as me. I'm really sorry Frankie had to get ill for us to become really good friends, but at least it made me realise everyone has their own personal struggles and no one is perfect.

BROTHERLY BOND: MALE TEENAGER

I'm fourteen and I have a girlfriend, although I'm not quite sure how that happened and I'm not quite sure I'm ready. I wasn't looking for a girlfriend. If I'm really honest, it was my mates egging me on, setting me up for a dare to ask her out. Well, I never step away from a dare or a challenge. Take last week in art, I was dared to get the whole class laughing at Miss Pitman. Challenge accepted. So, when Miss Pitman was walking around, I said, 'Miss, your laces are undone.' Well, immediately she looked down at her shoes and the whole class started laughing. I was immediately sent out and she couldn't get control of the class all lesson. You see, Miss Pitman our art teacher always wears sandals, she's a bit of a bohemian and the whole class knows that. Well, I got a detention and a telling off from Mum and Dad. To be honest I think I was unfairly treated, she should remember she's wearing sandals. Anyway, like I said, a dare's a dare and at lunch we were all in the gym, our gang one side and the girls on the other. Well, I got up walked over and asked Lucy to be my girlfriend. Her mates look amazed but not as amazed as I did when she said yes. All my mates jumped on top of me. I mean, I'm the first one to get a girlfriend out of our gang. So now I've got a girlfriend and, well, every night after school we go to the park and hang around the swings. My mates all fancy her mates and they like to come to the park too and try it on with them. Lucy's asked me not to keep bringing my mates to the park too, but why would I do that? I've told my mum and dad about Lucy. I don't have secrets from them, but I heard my mum tell my dad he needs to talk to me. Oh my god, this is so awkward. I know he'll be more embarrassed than me talking about sex. I think I'll just google anything I need to know or ask my mates.

IT'S NOT A CHOICE: FEMALE TEENAGER

Us lot know how to survive. Well, that's what everyone thinks. To some extent maybe they're right, because when I think about it you just have to get on with it. The worst night for me was when I woke up and some bloke was peeing on me. I just lay there in the doorway and froze. I just didn't know what to do. I've learnt though, you need to stick in twos and that way you don't get targeted as much and someone's always got your back. I need to get out of this though, I can't spend the rest of my life begging and being homeless. It's not a choice though, what else was I to do when I'd run away from home? I was only fifteen, well almost sixteen. You see I had to run away; I couldn't stand the abuse. My mum always had different men. They'd come and go but the last one, well, he stuck around, like a bad smell. She thought he loved her and who was I to break the illusion and tell her it was me he was mauling, me he'd be bothering most nights. It got to a point where I thought, what's worse, living in fear there or taking my chances out on the streets? I emptied his wallet and, well I came to London and I can tell you the streets aren't paved with gold, but I feel free out here. I met Martin about a month ago and he showed me a squat that a lot of homeless go to. He says with all these empty buildings there should be no need for people to be living on the streets. He's got a point. So, at night at least we feel safe, it's like a community here and people help you out. We even have electric, I'm not sure where from, but no running water. But you can't have everything for free and anyway, I do what they call the tramp's wash with baby wipes. You wash your bits and away you go. You can't be fussy. Do you see people offering to let us use their bathroom facilities, I don't think so? Martin says come the revolution the whole country will have to make change. He is really well educated. Some people say he's a rebel and when the revolution starts, he'll be leading. I just think he's kind and, in my life, I've not known much of that.

GROWING UP TOO QUICK: FEMALE TEENAGER

I was only twelve when my dad committed suicide. I still remember being told and I thought I'd never stop crying. I hurt so badly, and I couldn't stop feeling the pain. Mum and Dad were divorced, and Dad had re-married to Beverley who had two children from a previous marriage. I used to go and stay most weekends. I always felt that my dad was stuck in the middle, he was trying to please everyone and in the end he'd had enough. All kinds of scenarios were going round in my head, that maybe they had got it wrong and he was still going to collect me on Saturday morning as usual, but deep down I knew I was never going to see him ever again. At the funeral I felt like an outsider, I felt like I'd lost my link to the family. The atmosphere was strained. Everyone was trying to find someone to blame and there were lots of questions unanswered. People felt bitter and wanted to know why it was that a husband goes out in the evening and no suspicion was raised when he never returned. I was too young to understand fully, but the older I'm getting the more questions I've got niggling at me, as though I've a parasite inside eating away. Mum, well she's no use. Since she found out she just drinks day and night. In fact, I'm surprised her liver's still working. In the morning she'll get up and drink and when I come home from school, she's normally flat out. I mean passed out stone-cold drunk. I needed someone there for me but instead I was becoming my mum's carer. But she was so unhappy. I didn't feel I was the child anymore; I was growing up far too quickly. I read about the verdict online because that's what happens with suicide, a bunch of people give a verdict on how they think it happened. I know it's a joke, how can anyone know? It came to light years after that he was very unhappy in his marriage, had business worries and, even more disturbing, he'd actually been abused by a man when he was younger and the old guy had moved back to the area. Whatever your reasons, Dad, I'll try and understand, but I'm not sure I can as the way I see it nothing's worth leaving your daughter behind.

MOBILE PHONE: FE/MALE TEENAGER:

Have you taken my phone again? Why am I even asking? Of course you have, that's why I'm getting messages from ...*(phone beeps.)* Seriously, you put me on a dating site? How did you even do that when I'm not old enough? My mum checks my phone, seriously Jack, what is wrong with you? *(Phone beeps.)* Oh no, I'm getting messages and photos from random girls and boys. Oh my god, Jack, you've signed me up as bisexual. You are one sick dude. *(Phone beeps.)* Oh no, it's Mum. No, she's not sent me a photo and no she's not on the dating app. She wants to know why I've ordered ten pizzas to be delivered to school on my Go Henry card. *(Phone beeps.)* What is wrong with you? I only went to the toilet and you've got random girls and boys wanting to date me plus ten pizzas for lunch. It's not funny. *(Phone beeps.)* Sorry Miss Coward, it's my phone. I will turn it off now. You so owe me you moron, sometimes I wonder why we are friends? *(Phone beeps seven times)* Sorry, Miss, yes, I heard you. I'm putting it away. You've sent a block message to my entire phone contacts saying send money now, it's an emergency. I'm going to kill you Jack Robinson. Sorry, Miss, I can't get off Jack's head right now, because he's a plonker.

CARING: FEMALE TEENAGER

Sorry, I can't come to the park, or shopping, and sorry I'll have to decline your birthday invitation. Don't get me wrong, I'm not anti-social or suffering from agoraphobia, I just don't have time. Let me explain. My mum is really poorly and since Dad left I have to care for her and my two younger brothers. I suppose I'm my mum's main carer. My day starts really early when I have to get my mum's medication and then I make breakfast and get my brothers up and ready for school. Mum hates being a burden and she's always telling me, but I don't mind. I'd rather us all be together as a family. We've not heard from Dad in such a long time, well, since he left, and my younger brothers have taken it really bad and I don't blame them. That's one thing that really annoys me about adults – just because they fall out, why take it out on the children? I know Dad couldn't cope with Mum's illness but she didn't choose it and I'm sure she'd rather be out and about with her friends. Although saying that, all Mum's friends seem to have dropped off and stopped visiting since she became poorly. I always tell her that they couldn't have been real friends, as real friends stay loyal throughout your life, no matter what happens. Mum says I'm far too wise for my own good. I love school and although I'm busy at home I try and make time for all my schoolwork and I help my brothers with their homework. I think I'd like to be a teacher when I'm older but that all depends on Mum, as I can't go away to university and study, I mean who will look after her? Someone once said that people come and go but you'll only ever have one mum and that's why I'm looking after her. I love my family and as long as I can manage, we'll survive anything together.

PART OF THE PROBLEM: FE/MALE TEENAGER

I know black lives matter but don't all lives matter? What do you mean, I'm missing the point? Well, I don't see any difference between a black person or a white person. I treat all humans the same. Yeah, but just because loads of other people don't treat everyone the same, how's that my problem? What? Because I'm part of the problem? I just told you I don't have a problem with black people, in fact my cousin's black and it doesn't make any difference. What? To him it does? No, it doesn't, he's never said anything about feeling different or being treated different. My Nan always gets him the same presents as what she gets all her grandkids. His life experience is the same as mine. Well I think it is. Same family, same neighbourhood. Well, I've never asked him. Huh, the starting point is talking? What do you mean? No, I guess I don't know what it's like to be black, I just thought it'd be the same as being white. I tell you what, I'll talk to my cousin. I guess I've never really thought about it before. It doesn't affect me, so it's not bothered me. I get you now. That's the problem – it should bother me.

DON'T JUDGE ME: FEMALE TEENAGER

Do you know how many times I've heard the same thing shouted whilst I've been on the streets? 'You lot need to get a job and stop scrounging. All you lot do is drink and take drugs.' It gets even better – the council have put up signs 'beware vagrants.' It's almost laughable...almost. Is this how we treat our fellow human beings? I've been on the streets now for almost two years and I can tell you it doesn't get any easier. I can't even look up now when I'm begging, as I fear the eye contact with people. I'm getting so frustrated that my mental health is deteriorating. I've got a little girl and she's beautiful but having her has made me much weaker. Before I just had to care about myself but now I have her to think about and I think of her all the time. I can see you disapprove, I can see in your eyes what you're thinking. If only you had the guts to say what you're thinking. I'd hear you say, 'she should be sterllised, all these couples wanting a baby so badly and can't have one and she has one and then gives it up.' I'd then say to you, it won't be forever. *I'm going to get a place and a job, and I'll get my little girl back*. I made her that promise when social services took her, and I never break promises. You're all sat there judging me, don't deny it. I can see it in your eyes. I was once a happy teenager without a care in the world and then Mum got poorly. The doctors told us there was nothing they could do and she died. I can hear the doctors talking to my dad and saying, 'we made her as comfortable as possible.' Comfortable as possible, what's that all about? I was so angry, what had we done to deserve this? Why my mum? Dad was like a zombie. He couldn't cope, he lost his job and then one night he never came home. The first we heard was when the police came to the door asking for Mum and we had to tell them she'd passed away. Well, Dad had done the same, he'd put the hose pipe to the car and gassed himself. I just don't understand why he didn't take me with him, and then we could have all been together. He promised he'd always look after me. He lied. I'd lost both parents, in actual fact my whole family, within a month. So, don't judge me, as none of us know what's around the corner and anyone could end up like me, in your own space in the dark.

CHOICES: FE/MALE TEENAGER

Someone once told me, life's a journey, live it well. I was young and it made no sense but as I'm getting older, I'm starting to get what they meant. It's the choices you make that take you down different paths. The ups and downs of the windy roads. The ebb and flow of the sea's tide. One day you're stood on the top of the mountain looking down, feeling a swell of adrenaline, ecstasy, success and happiness, and the next you're careering down the hill, losing control. The brakes aren't working and you're falling, falling to the ground, when suddenly you get asked a question. It's just a yes or a no and in that moment you can keep hurtling down the hill waiting for the impact or you can come to a sudden halt, be thrown against the carriage wall and swing around the corner onto a level path. It's always your choice. It doesn't always feel that way but it's those small, insignificant moments where we make a choice. Yes, I'll do that or no I won't. They can change things so much and alter your journey, change your direction, send you spiralling out of control or raise you to new levels. I'm not saying things won't turn up in the road, people won't pull out on you, cut you up, crash into the back of you, but remember *you're driving*. They can crash into the back of you and you can drive away, or you can turn around and crash into them, and each time you do your vehicle is getting more damaged. Look after yourself, learn to drive better. I'm not saying the open well-maintained road is always the best, sometimes it's good to go off roading – challenge yourself – but think about the next step, where you want to get to, how you're going to get there. Drive to the top of that mountain and I'll meet you there.

DID ANYONE SEE?: FEMALE TEENAGER

I was happy it was the end of the school day. I'd been up to the shop with my friend and we were just walking to get on the bus. We turned the corner from the shop and all the school coaches were lined up on the street. As we walked briskly towards our coach, and two men were walking towards us probably in their twenties. I thought nothing of it as we went to walk by, laughing and joking, not a care in the world, but as we went by one of them grabbed me. He grabbed my chest. His hand squeezed tighter before releasing me. My body tensed and time stopped, before him and his friend laughed, and they carried on walking away. I carried on walking, shocked and disturbed. It was the briefest moment but it happened, and my friend turned to me and said, 'why didn't you knee him in the balls?' I didn't say anything. I looked at all the faces staring out from the coaches and thought about who was watching. Who just saw what happened? Were they thinking the same as my friend? I felt a bit funny. If I'm honest, I didn't know what I felt, and I never mentioned it to my friend or anyone again. It was only the briefest moment, just forget it and don't dwell. I just carried on like nothing happened, went home, had my tea, called round to my friend's and went home to bed. The next day I was happy it was the end of the school day. I'd been up to the shop with my friend and we were just walking to get on the bus. We turned the corner from the shop and all the coaches were lined up on the street. We walked briskly towards our coach and a boy from school was walking towards us and as he passed, I flinched. I physically jumped. I felt a shudder run through me, a fear, an unease, a cold crawling discomfort up my spine. It only lasted for the briefest moment but it was there, an awkward, uncomfortable rush. It was only in that second, I realised that yesterday's briefest moment that I'd shrugged off would affect me for much longer. To the guy it was just a quick joke, a laugh, friends messing about, daring each other, the briefest moment, it meant nothing. To me it meant I didn't trust everyone, I didn't feel at ease with everyone, I wasn't comfortable with people coming towards me. Every time I turned that corner, I relived it. It was only the briefest moment, but it changed me.

DRUNKEN NIGHT OUT: FEMALE TEENAGER

I'm so happy, woohoo! Because I'm happy, I'm happy, I'm glad it's over, I'm glad *(laughter turns to tears)* it's over. Ahhh...Esther...I'm all alone now. No one wants me. I'm like Princess Jasmine without my Aladdin. I'm Lady without my Tramp. And if that dirty, dirty, tramp, that dirty scrubber, hadn't thrown herself at my bae I'd still be his princess. His babe. His pretty girl. You, you take your cheap dirty gutterslut and your cheating twiggy legs and walk away. Don't look back with your dirty eyes. Your dirty cheating eyes. This is what you could have had. This is what you could have had. Woohoo! Because I'm happy. Take your dirty cheating legs and your dirty cheating arms and...and dirty cheating hands, your cheating feet, your cheating ugly toenails, and...and your dirty cheating, cheating ugly... *(mumbling more and more.)* Home? Home? Esther, Esther pester, I don't wanna go home. I wanna go partty! Paaarrrtty! *(Collapses.)*

DATING APP: MALE TEENAGER

Lisa Attwood asked me out. She's probably the best-looking girl in the school but about as intelligent as Joey Essex. I made a comment about her weak gene pool and needing someone who can at least do basic multiplication. A bit harsh, but I think she thought I was talking about going swimming in denims and she just stared at me in a beautifully vacant fashion as I made my get away. That's what I made out anyway, but actually the truth is I'm gay. I've kissed girls for show, but I might as well have been kissing a toilet bowl. I felt nothing but horror. I'm pretty gorgeous, if I do say so myself, so I can get away with appearing picky. I did tell my mum I was gay, but she just said don't be so dramatic, Jonathan, you're just like your father. That told me a lot about their relationship and maybe even where I get my tendencies from. I haven't bothered telling anyone else since. Well, apart from those viewing my Grindr profile. I've had a lot of interest which is understandable, but I've not met anyone yet, but by tomorrow I'll no longer be a virgin. Well, a Grindr dating virgin, I'm not easy darling. I'm going to meet dirtygarry. I think it's supposed to be a pun on Dirty Harry, although I hope he's not a copper as theoretically I shouldn't be on Grindr, you're supposed to be eighteen to use the site but hey ho, let's give it a go. We're meeting at a park in town. There'll be loads of people about so if he's not a ten I'll just say no thank you and leave. What's the worst that can happen?

WHAT'S THE WORST THAT CAN HAPPEN?: MALE TEENAGER

I'm Jonathan. I was raped. I didn't report it. I was so ashamed. I'm disgusted in myself. I should have done more. I shouldn't have got into that situation. I always thought I was intelligent but now I know I'm just some pathetic loser. I thought I'd be safe. I said to myself, what's the worst that can happen? Well, now I know. I thought I was in control of the situation but now I realise it was his plan all along. He wanted to rape me from the start, or maybe he thought I'd just want sex. We met on Grindr. He looked genuine and was, well, he was gorgeous. We messaged and arranged to meet. He turned up and he looked just as fit as his photo. We talked for a bit in the park where we met and then he said he'd forgot his wallet and he'd have to nip home and then we'd go for some food. He asked me to join him. He seemed so nice and we were getting on. So, I said yes. He'd parked his car a few streets away and we set off to his. We arrived at his house and he asked me to go in with him. He said his flat mates were out and he'd probably be ages looking for his wallet. I thought nothing of it. We went inside and he started looking around for his wallet before he called me into the back room, which turned out to be a bedroom. I guessed his bedroom. He grabbed hold of me and started touching me. I told him to hang on and he let go of me. He asked me if I wanted sex. I said no and he just changed. He grabbed me again but he really forcibly grabbed me, he grabbed me hard. He started to drag my top off. He was a lot stronger than me. He held my arms above my head as he ripped my t-shirt off. I was petrified, my voice stopped working. I tried to fight but it was no use, he was so strong and forceful. The more I struggled the more violent he became. I just submitted. I was so weak I just gave in. He started undoing my trousers and I couldn't do anything. I was frozen with fear. He asked me if I was ok with it and I remember I shook my head as tears rolled from my eyes, but I couldn't get my words out, I didn't make a sound, I didn't fight. My body just gave up. He did what he wanted with me after that. I was like a doll. A piece of meat. The pain was intense, but the fear was numbing. After what seemed like forever, he finally stopped and left me naked strewn across the bed as he'd placed me. At first, I couldn't move. I felt so embarrassed, ashamed, vulnerable, scared. I wanted to pretend I didn't exist, but I could feel his eyes on me which added to the humiliation lying there naked with him looking over me. I didn't move until I heard him leave the room and I rushed to grab my clothes. I sat on the bed facing the wall in silence before he came back in and said he'd give me a lift back to town. I don't know whether it was the shock or the fear or the fact I'm just such a loser, but I said yes. I couldn't look at him, it was like I was ashamed of what just happened and he was fine with it. He'd totally exploited me. He'd seen me at my most vulnerable and that gave him the power and I just felt shame. He just seemed the same as before, it meant nothing to him. He dropped me where we met, and I got the bus home. I was a cocky, self-assured seventeen-year-old before and now I'm just a scared, pathetic little boy. I can't cope with how I feel. I can't cope with this in my mind. I feel dirty all the time. I just feel disgusted in myself and I can't cope. I don't know how to handle this. I'm so weak. I'm such a failure. I disgust myself.

IT'S EASIER TO SAY NOTHING: MALE TEENAGER

Brad's a bit intense sometimes. He's just got into all this British National stuff. He keeps telling me they're going to get rid of all the foreigners from our country. I'm not sure foreigners really even bother me. His dad says they're taking all our jobs and ruining our country, but my mum and dad have both got jobs, and they don't seem that bothered by foreigners. I'm a bit worried I'm friends with a racist. I mean, he's a nice guy when he's not going on about foreigners and ethnic minorities. Sometimes he even starts on queers. Thinking about what I just said he sounds like a right idiot, but I've known him all my life and well, he's alright some of the time. Actually, it's a bit worrying because I guess someone felt the same way about Hitler. I sometimes tell Brad I'm not interested. Maybe I should tell him the way he talks about people disgusts me, but I can't really be bothered arguing about it. Is that what all Hitler's friends thought? Yeah, ok, that's a strange idea Adolf about the gas chambers, but do you fancy a kick about? Hey Adolf, I didn't think you were that serious about all this war business, but anyway shall we go get a bratwurst? You've invaded Poland? Oh, yeah, but I'll forgive you because it was hilarious when we were kids and we water bombed Mr Shindler. Yeah, maybe I need to stand up for what I believe in as much as he does. I don't want to be party to the next Hitler. I don't want to be a war criminal because I just couldn't be bothered to put my point across. I don't want him telling people I agree with him because it was easier to say nothing. I guess next time I have to say something, or I'm no better than him, and if it means we can't be friends, then maybe he's not the right person to be friends with.

I CAN'T BELIEVE SHE'S GONE: FE / MALE TEENAGER

We grew up together and got up to all sorts with each other. She always seemed to be there when I got up to mischief and she always seemed to know when I was down and needed a cuddle. She was one of my best friends. She did everything for me and asked for nothing back, just love, and I really did love her. I can't believe she's gone. I don't know what I'll do without her. I'm going to really miss her. Mum was so upset she locked herself in her bedroom for the afternoon after giving herself a migraine. Dad even had to cook tea. It's like everywhere I turn I expect to see her, but she's just gone and it's so sad. Some people don't understand, and they can be really hurtful. She might have been only a dog to them, but she was family to me. She'd been with me as I grew up, she'd made me smile and laugh, loved me when I was sad, played out with me growing up. Got in trouble with me and been a true friend. If you've had a dog, you'd understand, but until then don't tell me she was just a dog. I loved her and she loved me and that's really special.

ARE YOU LISTENING?: FE / MALE TEENAGER

Come on in. Welcome to my waiting room. You'll soon be entering the wonderful world of worry. Take a seat. Bite your nails. Pull your hair. Pace back and forth. Let your mind play tricks on you. When you pass through those doors you will face your biggest anxiety. Will you make it to the other side? What is it that worries you? Can you feel your heart rate rising? Is your breathing getting shallow? Are you ready to face your fears? Can you control your nerves? Are you prepared for panic attacks? Are you in control of your mind or is your mind in control of you? It's going to be frightening. In fact, it's going to be unbearable. Only the brave, the risk takers, the fearless, the confident, the controlled, will make it. It's not for life's losers. Remember, you don't have to do it. Let's start the countdown. Five, four, three, two, one. Let the doors open. Now, deep breaths and walk into your worries. Can you do it? Where will the world of worries take you? I wouldn't dare if I were you. You don't look like you'll make it. Hang on. Don't do it. Hey, don't all leave me. Come back, you'll never make it. Are you listening? It's going to be terrible! Don't do it! Don't face your fears. Stay here with me where it's safe. Stay here in the waiting room. Don't take the big step. Don't do it. Come back to me. You'll embarrass yourself. You'll fail. Everyone will see you're a loser. Come back to me. Come back to me. Come back to my safety. Don't leave me. Don't do it.

TELLING MUM AND DAD: MALE TEENAGER

All my friends tell me people are open minded these days. Nobody cares any more. Well, that's easy for them to say. They don't have to tell their mum and dad they're gay. It's alright Dad being open minded about James down the street being a puff. He laughs and says James is ok as long as you keep your back to the wall. Or Emily being one of them lesbians, but she was such a pretty little girl, as my mum says. I know they're not hateful people, but I also know it's not what they want to hear. I'm their only son. My dad always wanted a boy after having my two older sisters and then he got me, what a let down. I've been trying all my life to make my dad and my mum proud, but I know this is going to be a disappointment to them both. I know it's not going to be a joyous coming out and I'm dreading having to do it. Do I even need to do it? My friends keep telling me I need to tell them but do I really? Do my friends just want the drama? I mean, none of them care, the girls all love having a gay friend. I'm like the essential fashion accessory. I just don't think Mum and Dad will see it like that. Von says they probably already know but I'm not so sure. The main reason I'm really considering telling them is because of Mike. We've been seeing each other for a couple of months and I'm really happy when we're together and I just want my mum and dad to meet him. I know they'd like him as much as I do but I don't know whether I'd rather just keep things the way they are. Although can I cope with Nan asking me again when I'm going to get myself a nice girlfriend, Dad giving me pep talks on how to treat women and Mum telling me not to treat my girlfriends like my dad treats her. Yeah, I think it's easier that way and I'm not letting anyone down, well, apart from myself and Mike.

COOLOMETER: MALE TEENAGER

I just want to be cool, but every time I try it all ends up going wrong. I'd say I'm socially awkward. All the cool boys, guys, brothers, road men, mandem, actually I'm that out of the loop, I don't even know what to call them, but I want to be like them. Cycling on their bikes, hands free, looking at their mobiles, doing wheelies and giving all the girls a nod. I tried to casually ride my bike through the school gates last week and I just didn't even achieve a single mark on the cool scale. In fact, I'd say I put myself into the minus figures. I almost crashed into Corey Thompson as I came through the gate, swerved to miss him and wobbled pathetically into a bush. It wasn't even a crash and screech of brakes, just a wobble and a flop. I decided to walk the next day. I just seem to have one main talent in life – to humiliate myself. On Tuesday there was a rap battle at school and for some reason I ended up involved. I've got to be one, if not the most, un-rap, hip hop, street bluds in the whole school. Robbie Stoker pulled me into the circle and started spitting bars at me. He said something like, 'sad, skunk chunk specky beak, low down, loser, spotty geek. Snide, two stripe trainers, Primark chic. Boy makes Peppa Pig look on fleek.' Now I'm supposed to say something back to that. Everyone's clicking their fingers and cheering, and I'm stood there with a whirlwind of words in my head and for some reason the only topic I picked up on was Peppa Pig. My reply went something like. 'Grandma piggy and George went out, they heard an ugly pig give a shout, about Peppa Pig being on fleek, and they said look at the state of you, you've got some cheek.' It didn't really even make sense and it proved I knew all about Peppa Pig, but actually the crowd seemed to like it, so I carried on. 'Have you met the mum of Robbie Stoker? She's so dirty, I wouldn't poke her, her face looks like the back end of the joke-' and bam, he punched me in the face. I guess I got a bit carried away. I fell to the ground like a big girl and the cool points I'd just earned were wiped straight out *(makes noise like points being wiped out on a game)*. *(Computer type voice)* You have lost all your points, please start again, and I've now got Robbie Stoker and his gang on my case, although I have had a couple of people click their fingers at me and say 'respect' so maybe I have moved out of the minus figures on the coolometer.

AN ORDINARY BOY: MALE TEENAGER

I want to be a hero. I grew up loving superheroes. Batman, Spiderman, Superman, the Hulk, all of them. I always wanted to be one. I think this is as close as I'll get. Fighting for my country, saving lives. Outwitting evil. I don't really agree with war and that's the point. I need to go to war to end war. We need to fight and destroy the evil. A band of brothers sacrificing their safety for their country, for their children, for their children's children. I joined the cadets and I thought, *yes this is it*. I made some great friends and it was fun and we were always safe. So, I signed up and I've been accepted to the army. I've got my chance to be a true hero. I want to be a hero but it's sinking in now. I'm not a superhero. I don't have a special power. I'm just a young lad who wants to save the world. A kid who loved the cadets and wanted to do something with his life. But now I'm really going to war. War. War like you see on the news, you read about in the papers, you watch on films, and I've no superpower, just myself and my brothers, and when we get ambushed it'll be real bullets, it'll be real bombs, we won't be safe. The officer won't explain what just happened and say what we could have done better or differently. We'll get one chance and if someone shouts *man down* it's real. They're really injured. It's not pretend. It's not a bag stuffed with whatever, a plastic target, it's a real human being, a real life, a son or a daughter that will bleed real blood. A life that can be taken, a body that can die. It's suddenly really dawned on me I'm not a hero, I'm just an ordinary man, an ordinary boy, and I don't know if I'm cut out for helping save the world.

MY DAD WAS SPECIAL TOO: FE/MALE TEENAGER

He died the same day as Nelson Mandela, and I hated Nelson Mandela for that. It was all over the news, everyone going on about Nelson Mandela and I wanted to tell them my dad was more important than Nelson Mandela. I don't care about Nelson Mandela. It should be my dad on the news. My dad was special too. My dad was a great man. He did a lot to help people. My dad was loved my many, but no one was bothered about my dad. He didn't make the news, no, just Nelson Mandela, Nelson Mandela, Nelson Mandela. Like he was the only person that died that day. I've been angry at Nelson Mandela ever since. I mean, I know it's not his fault, I know he was an amazing man who achieved so much but so was my dad and I wanted it to be about my dad, but all everyone was bothered about was Nelson Mandela. Everyone told me I'd feel sad when Dad died, no one told me I'd feel angry. The only good that came out of it is that I looked really intelligent when Mrs Broadbent asked when Nelson Mandela died in class the other day and then I was really annoyed with myself for answering because why were we learning about him again and no one was asking about my dad. I shouldn't have answered, I shouldn't have honoured his memory by answering. I put myself in a really bad mood and I couldn't explain why to anyone. One, because they wouldn't understand, and two, because I'd have to mention flaming Nelson Mandela again.

IMAGE OF ME: MALE TEENAGER

Al in our class says he was born in the wrong body. He reckons he should be a girl and I get that because I think I was born in the wrong body too. I mean, who'd think my scrawny body was the right one for anyone? I'm not going to admit to thinking this is the right body for me. I think I should've been born in the body of some tall, ripped, good-looking babe magnet, if I'm honest. I mean, I've got the moves, I've got the style, I've got the chat and I've definitely got class but then the girls look at me and are like *where's that cool mofo I was messaging*. I try and style it out, but I think they can see past my swagger. Girls love me but always just as a friend and I blame this body. I was watching *Blind Date* with my gran the other night and I thought, *yeah, if I was answering the questions then I'd be the pick of the chicks*. My gran agreed, but I know deep down when Paul O'Grady said, 'and here he is, it's Lee, the greatest guy you'll ever meet,' the girl'd be like, 'nah that ain't the dude I picked, he sounded so cool.' I am cool, I've just been born in the wrong body. That image you've got in your head, stick with it because that's the real me. Al said he can get help on the NHS. I'm wondering if I could too. Maybe I could get peck implants. Leg lengthening must be a thing, right? I'm thinking the doc's the way forward. Maybe I could get some testosterone shots if Al can get oestrogen. A nose job, chiselled jaw. There's got to be some help somewhere for a cool dude trapped in a wimp's body in this day and age, otherwise all the girls are just going to keep missing out on the best catch in town.

DO YOU BLAME ME?: FEMALE TEENAGER

A teacher has just had to stop Leah attacking another pupil. The teacher is trying to calm Leah down, reason with her and understand the issue.

Get off me, I don't care, I don't freaking care. I hate her, I freaking hate her...I don't want to be calm...I don't want to calm down. I want to finish her, I want to wipe the smug grin off her face, smash her smirk in. I hate her, I hate her. And...I'm supposed to care? Murder... yeah, but she's not dead. I wish she was. Why? Why? Because she's evil and she's made my life hell for over a year. I did tell someone. I told my form teacher, and do you know what she said? *Keep away from her – avoid her*. I didn't want to see her. I never wanted to see her, but she'd make a point of seeing me every morning. Every single morning she'd be waiting, her and her smug mates. Do you know what it's like to have someone tell you you're useless, push you, shove you, tell you you're ugly, call you a freak, every single day? I did walk away. I walked away every day. I let them laugh at me, rob me, shove me around every single day and do you know what? I'd had enough. Do you blame me? Do you really blame me? It's her fault she's in hospital cause she's evil...I did, I told my mum, and do you know what she said? Keep away from her, don't let her see she's getting to you, she'll get bored, just as long as it doesn't affect your education. But she didn't get bored, she kept on every day. You freak, you freak, you freak, you freak, and I looked into her face this morning and she smirked, and they all laughed, and I just grabbed her. I slapped her, I punched her, I pulled her hair and her so called friends, they did nothing. Do you know why? Because they know she deserved it. I just couldn't stop once I'd started. I just kept hitting her, once for every time she'd hurt me. I would have just kept going if you hadn't stopped me 'cos I hate her, I hate her, I really hate her, and if she died at least I wouldn't have to see her smug face every morning. And now you all want to know, now you all care. I just couldn't put up with it anymore, I couldn't go on with it every day, I was tired and no one would help me, and do you know why it hurt so much? Because she's right. She's right, I am a sad, lonely, ugly freak. I know it. I don't want to be reminded every day. I didn't need her to keep telling me. What do you mean I'm not? I know I am. She's told me every day for over a year and you telling me once that I'm not a freak, well...I don't believe you. I know she's right and I hate myself. I hate myself as much as I hate her.

YOU'RE NO FRIEND: FEMALE TEENAGER

Oi, Nina...Nina...Nina Connors, don't ignore me. Get over here. Are you ignoring me? Is she ignoring me? After what that rat's been up to. She's just going to ignore me now. You weren't ignoring me when you were grassing me up. No, not much to say now, have you? You snake. You two-faced snake. It was your idea in the first place. You were the one telling me to do it. You said we'd never get caught. What you meant was, if we do, you'll grass me up and get yourself off. You've took me for a right mug. Well, now it's time to get my own back. What you saying? Are you serious? Are you for real? I'm supposed to believe you didn't say a thing. Yeah right. Who was it then? The invisible man? You can't save yourself now, it's too late. What do you think, Ali, do we believe her? No, you're no friend. You've been exposed, you're a fake. Shut it. Hold her against that wall. I'm going to make myself feel better. By the time I'm done with this rat she'll be lying in the gutter where she belongs.

LOST IN THE MOMENT: FEMALE TEENAGER

Picture it. It's Friday afternoon, Mr Bolton has been called out of the room for some reason or other, we didn't know why. Well we're all just whispering, and we start talking about the weekend. There's only like forty-five minutes to go and we'll be free from school for two whole days. So Amber starts playing Blinding Lights by The Weekend on her phone. Woooh, tune! It's been ages since Mr Bolton left and we're supposed to just sit and carry on working. Like yeah, right. So, I stands up and starts singing and dancing along – and then Flo joins in and we're getting lost in the moment. Everyone's singing and feeling alive and we climbs on the desk and we're singing, 'I'm running out of time,' when we realises the music has died and it's all quiet and everyone else is sat down. We turn to face the door slowly and not only is Mr Bolton stood there but Mrs Bolshaw, the headmistress, is standing there too. Oh no! I have lots of conflicting thoughts in my head. Do I look like I don't care? Do I try and sit down really slowly, and they might not even notice I'm moving? Do I start jumping and pretend I'm trying to remove a cobweb from the ceiling? *Lola Howard and Floella Allen, my office now!* Too late, all my tactical reactions are too slow. Next decision – how to style out climbing down from a desk when the whole class is watching.

COMING OUT: FEMALE TEENAGER

I told my mum and dad I was gay last week. It didn't go as well as I thought. They were both heartbroken, they actually cried. I mean, Matt's mum wasn't fazed at all and Jen's mum said she already knew. My mum and dad said they already knew but I think they'd rather I lived a lie and kept things normal. They cried, saying that I'd never get married and have children. I mean, I might not if I was straight, but when I explained about gay marriage and sperm donation it didn't seem to ease the hysteria. It was like I'd told them I was terminally ill. It was like they'd lost me. Dad even put a photo of me as a child next to his bed, as if he was physically grieving. I saw it when I went to borrow Mum's straighteners, it'd never been there before. I mean, they didn't kick me out or anything like some parents do. They didn't demand I wasn't gay. They were just really sad, and things have been different between us. They didn't really mention it again, they've just been distant and weird, well, until yesterday when Mum asked me if I had a girlfriend. I was caught off guard and I just blurted out about Jen, and then she said they wanted to meet her. I was proper freaked out. Would they be nice to her? Would they like her? Would they blame her? What did they want to meet her for? Well, today's the day, I'm taking Jen round for tea. Mum said this morning her and Dad were both really looking forward to it. I went in the bedroom and the photo of me had gone. They both gave me a really big hug before I left for school this morning and it was like, things were back to normal. I don't know why or what's happened or if they just needed time, but I think it's going to be ok and I'm actually quite excited for them to meet Jen.

IN THE NAME: MALE TEENAGER

Meet my brothers, Kaden and Jaden. They are always getting into trouble and Mum spends most of her time lying and trying to protect them as the police hammer down the door to our house. Grandma says they're a pair of wronguns, just like Dad. Aidan, that's my dad, is in prison for his fourth, or is it fifth, time. I can't remember a time in my life when I've not visited someone in prison. Grandma says it's not worth the taxi fare home from the prison as he's back in days or sometimes even hours later. He tells me that he's out to collect his supplies. I really don't know what he means. Mum says to Kayden and Jaden, *if you don't start behaving, you'll be in a cell next to your Dad*. They think it'll be like a chalet at Butlins. You see, Dad tells them it's like a holiday camp. I'm not sure Dad's got that right. He says, *no son, you don't pay any bills, you watch television all day, go to the gym and earn more money inside than you do outside*. I can't see that myself, but unlike my brothers I don't intend to find out. I'm just going to quietly study away and try and make a life away from crime – it's not easy though. Everyone says it's in the name and they seem to tar all of us with the same brush. So, there's Dad, Aidan, shortly followed by my brothers, Jayden and Kaden, and well, I really don't fit in with them as I'm called Dave, or do they mean our surname, Pratt, that'll be it then.

PRACTICAL JOKERS: FE/MALE TEENAGER

I'm seriously not going in that water. It's disgusting. Look, there's all green floating on the top. I read the other week that you shouldn't swim in rivers, it's dangerous. I'm not joking. It said the dangers of strong underwater currents can cause trouble for the most confident swimmers. It also said the water can be colder than you think and cause shock. Look, I'm not a wuss, I'm trying to be sensible. Will you all stop laughing at me. Look, don't put your head under the water, you can catch things. Will you be serious? I don't mean catch fish, you can get sick, rivers can be contaminated with sewage and wastewater. Oh, I'm going home. I've had enough of you making fun of me. Bye, see you, wouldn't wanna be you. No, I'm not coming back; you can shout all you like. Seriously, you're going to play the *oh look I'm drowning routine*. Not falling for that one again. No, I can't hear you. I'm off to my nice, warm, comfortable house. What, what's wrong? Are you being serious, of course you're not, you're just messing around like last time and the time before, so I jump in to save you both and then you both get out and pinch all my clothes. No, not happening, not again. You're not fooling me again. Look, seriously keep your mouth closed, seriously you'll swallow water and make yourself sick. You're being serious, aren't you? Look, I'll be right back, I'll try and get help. No, I can't jump in, we'll all be dragged down together. Hang on, I'm calling for help. Oh no, there's no signal. Look, I'm going to run this way and find signal. Hold on, someone's coming to help. Jason, Kelvin, stop messing around. Help's on its way. Jason, Kelvin, where are you?

SAME DIFFERENCE: MALE TEENAGER

Did you hear what he just called you blud? What, you're just gonna ignore it? What is wrong with you, man? Nobody is gonna speak to me like that. What do you mean, leave it? What are you on? Look we can't stand for this no longer, I'm tired of crossing the street, being the wrongun. Times are changing and if you don't stand for what's right, then you might as well roll over and let them kick you so hard that you bleed, man. This shit is real. I've had enough of being spoken to like I'm something on the bottom of their shoe. Maybe you're happy with that, maybe that's alright by you. Nah, it's not good enough for me anymore. Why should we be treated differently from the next man? Tell me, what's the difference? We are equal, gone are the days of slavery. Everyone was created equal and that's how we should all live. I'm sick of it. Don't create any trouble, do your best to fit in. Well, if being spat at and abused is fitting in, then I am going to create, and I am going to protest and I am going to fight for what I believe. I believe in a world where everyone is born equal and should have the same respect as the next person, no matter about the colour of skin, whether they be rich or poor. People deserve respect and should be able to live a life without aggro and prejudice.

TOILET TROUBLE: FEMALE TEENAGER

Oh, that's much better. I can't believe Miss Stowe wouldn't let me out of class to go to the toilet. You'd think as a biology teacher she'd have sympathy for the human body and its needs. Oh no, I don't believe it, there's no loo roll left. I should have checked before I came in. I normally always check and then swap cubicles. Right, I need a plan of action. What about if I check in my bag first. I don't believe this. I've only gone and left my bag in biology in the rush to get to the toilet. Oh god, what am I going to do now? My phone, I'll text Maisie, she'll come down and throw me some loo roll over. I don't believe it, no reception. Oh, for goodness sake, should I just call 999? Oh, pull yourself together Georgia, this isn't a major emergency. Well, at least the toilets are empty, so I'll just have to sneak into another cubicle. Ok...one...two...three...go! Made it! Oh, for goodness sake, there's no loo roll in here either. This is ridiculous. Oh, I can hear someone, maybe it's the cleaner. Excuse me, excuse me. Oh no, it's Karen Miller, of all the people my arch enemy. No, I'm fine, I just felt a bit sick watching that frog being dissected in biology. No, I'll stay here for a little bit longer. I'm fine, honestly. Yes, I know the toilets stink, yes somebody must have taken a really big smelly dump, I hear what you're saying. Ok, bye, see you later. I don't believe this; the bell is going to go in five minutes and the toilets will be full. Oh no, someone else has come in. Oh, thank goodness, it's Miss Harvey. *Miss, I've got a bit of a problem, there's no toilet roll in any of the toilets.* Would it be possible for you to get me some please? Well, nothing prepared me for what came next. Miss Harvey shoutss, 'Karen Miller, can you please go to the caretaker's office and collect some toilet roll for Georgia Temple please.' She replied, 'Of course Miss Harvey, I thought Georgia was sick. I didn't realise it was her who'd stunk the toilets out with a huge dump.'

I WANT MY MUM, I DON'T WANT TO DIE: FE/MALE TEENAGER

I want my mum, I don't want to die. I want my mum, I don't want to die. I want my mum, I don't want to die. He said it over and over, he looked terrified. I could only comfort him. I'll never forget what I saw. They slashed his side and knifed him around his chest. I tried to stem the bleeding. The person that died was his mum's only child and that child's not here anymore. They are absolutely devastated. They cannot believe their son has gone. This senseless loss has affected the whole community. A parent's worst nightmare. I heard them, they shouted, 'Get him from the other side. Get him from the other side.' She shouted, 'Don't kill him.' I tried to stem the bleeding. I asked him twice if he knew them – he said no. He was still alive when I got to him and he spoke – that's the saddest part. *I want my mum, I don't want to die. I want my mum, I don't want to die. I want my mum, I don't want to die.* They carry knives for protection. They want pride. They put their parents through hell. They must be so ashamed. Would they ever think their son could be capable of such violence. A moment of madness. If they could turn the clock back, would they? They must think about these things. They must come back to haunt them. An unprovoked attack. I asked him twice if he knew them – he said no. He was still alive when I got to him and he spoke – that's the saddest part. *I want my mum, I don't want to die. I want my mum, I don't want to die. I want my mum, I don't want to die.* Flashback and nightmares. I can't escape what happened. He had a girlfriend. She loved him. He was her first real boyfriend. She lived next door to him. Everyone says he took the time to say hello. He was an intelligent boy who showed real potential to succeed in life. I know people who are carrying knives right now, they say it's a risk they've just got to take because the penalty is get killed or go to prison. If you've got no bodies on your blade, who even are you? Rambo, ramsey, shank. It's just banter. Just banter. They got someone for it. He denies murder. He'd been stabbed six times and there were defensive injuries on his hands from trying to take control of the blade. Pathologists found the proximity of the chest wounds were consistent with a rapid sequence of infliction and indicated the use of substantial force. He didn't take a knife out that night to use it. He didn't intend to kill him, but he did. Now he's in jail for life. Living with the feeling that he's taken a life – it can't be nice. Especially when you're in your cell, on your own, all night, and you've got nothing else to do. Just thirty seconds later, your whole life's different. My life and so many others. The friends he had run with, the witnesses, the witnesses' families, his parents, my parents, our families, the community. Lives will never be the same and the victim doesn't have a life at all. I saw him repeatedly stabbing a boy who lay on the floor. I've been affected very deeply by it. I tried to stem the bleeding. I asked him twice if he knew them – he said no. He was still alive when I got to him and he spoke – that's the saddest part. *I want my mum, I don't want to die. I want my mum, I don't want to die. I want my mum, I don't want to die.*

START A REVOLUTION: FE/MALE TEENAGER

People are always telling me to stop going on about climate change and pollution. Not just kids, adults too. I get it all the time. People seem more concerned about what's happening to make-believe characters in the soaps than what's happening to our world. It makes me crazy. Are people so stupid? I wish I went to school with Greta Thunberg and then at least one person in my class would actually be on the same wavelength as me. My school's just full of dim, narrow-minded sheep, who want to be like all these fake reality stars with tacky personalities, no morals and a single brain cell between ten of them. So, I told my mum I was going to be like Greta. *Uh huh*, she nodded. *Yes love*. I don't even think she knew who Greta was and she didn't really care, she was just humouring me. So, I skipped school and sat outside the council building with my banner saying 'school strike for climate' just like Greta. And just like Greta there was just me on my own because all my classmates think I'm a bit of a weirdo. I sat there all day waiting for that moment when the world starts taking me seriously, but it never happened. I shouted 'school strike for climate' at a few people who just looked bewildered or smirked as if to say, *who does that kid she think she is?* I went home feeling like a total failure. I don't think I've got it in me to be the next Greta. I guess that's why she's so amazing. I'm just an ordinary girl who hates what we're doing to the world. It takes more than that to start a revolution – and I got a detention and I got grounded. How am I supposed to save the world when no one will listen to me?

DRAMA EXERCISES

Simple ideas to help young actors perform their monologues

CREATING YOUR CHARACTER

It's always good to get to know your character in a monologue to help with your performance. Fill in the answers to become familiar with your character.

Character's Name:	
Character's Age:	
Character's Voice/Accent:	
Character's Physicality: Look at posture, walk, distinguishing features.	
Character's Occupation:	
Character's Interests:	
Character's Beliefs:	
Character's Ambition:	
Character's favourite colour:	
Character's favourite food:	
Character's favourite movie:	

Character's favourite animal:	
Character's song that you would use to signify this monologue:	
Where does your character live?	
An item associated with your character:	
Does your character have any similarities to you?	
Does your character have any differences to you?	
Who is your character talking to? What is your relationship? (You would talk differently to a friend than a teacher or parent.)	
Your feelings towards other characters mentioned:	
Does your character have any obstacles to overcome?	
List your characters change in emotion throughout the monologue:	

VOCAL WARM UP

It's always important to warm up your voice if you are going to be speaking a lot. Tension in many parts of the body can result in a voice that is strained or lacking in full tonal quality, therefore tension release exercises are a vital part of your vocal warm up.

Hips

- Wiggle hips from side to side or rotate in big circular motions.

Shoulders

- Roll shoulders backwards and forwards.
- Shrug shoulders, hold breath and tense muscles down the arms to the finger tips. Release on a big sigh.

Neck

- Roll head along chest to look over one shoulder then roll back across chest to the other shoulder. Keep breathing throughout.
- Looking up at ceiling and down to floor. Repeat.

Facial muscles, jaw, lips and tongue (Articulators)

- Massage and/or tap face.
- Stretch face into its widest position then scrunch up as tight and small as possible.
- Chew imaginary toffee.
- Protrude lips then stretch wide.
- Massage jaw muscle at the point between the back teeth.
- Roll tongue in circles around the front of the teeth. Start off doing four times in one direction and then the other, followed by three times, twice, then once each way. By the end the neck may ache (part of the tongue is connected down here) so a massage may help.

FRICATIVES

Help to prevent the voice sounding strained.

Fricative sounds include: 'vvvv' and 'zzzzz'

- Imagine you are a motorbike.
- Rev the engine on these sounds.
- You should notice the tummy button bounce inwards as you rev (note that the top of the stomach and sides of abdomen above the hips should move outwards. These are key support muscles for the breath).
- Try this exercise on different pitches throughout the range.
- You can then open out from the fricative into vowels (A,E,I,O,U) and sustain.

DRAMA EXERCISES

SOUND IT

On your own you are going to read your monologue but not with the words. Instead, you are going to only use sounds. You must still get the same emphasis and meaning but you can only use sound. To start with only use one sound for the whole monologue. Once that's complete you can introduce a few sounds and maybe a different sound for a different emotion. It's a fun game and can produce amazing results as you are concentrating on the sounds and not so much the words.

PHYSICALIZE IT

To be carried out in pairs or individually and in front of a mirror if possible. After studying your character, you are going to think about the physicality of the character. You are going to concentrate on how your character:

- Shakes Hands
- Drinks
- Eats
- Uses a phone
- Reads a magazine
- Brushes their hair
- Brushes their teeth

There are lots of everyday tasks that we do naturally. Throughout your day think about how your monologue's character would perform these tasks differently.

SAY MY LINE

Take a sentence from your monologue. Think of three different ways to say the sentence by altering your tone of voice, speed, volume or pitch. This can be repeated with several lines to help you realise the differing emphasis that can be placed on each sentence.

SECRET MONOLOGUE

Deliver the monologue using a stage whisper and occasionally look over your shoulder to see if anyone is listening.

Next: Keep using the stage whisper as though it's a secret you're sharing with the audience. This time look over your shoulder, stand up and check either side of the room to see if anyone is there listening and then continue with the monologue.

This exercise will help get the intensity into the monologue.

ADVERTISEMENT

Once you are familiar with the character and their background in the monologue, the next exercise is an advert. In character you are going to decide if your character was on television or a market stall or even the radio, what would your character advertise? When you've thought of a product, come up with an advertising slogan, a brief yet memorable phrase for example:

- *Have a break, Have a Kit Kat*
- *Just do it*
- *I'm Lovin' it*

Think of the emotion in the slogan, this should be the same emotion as is in your monologue.

VOLUME BUTTON

A simple yet effective exercise to help a performer's concentration.

Working in pairs to perform your monologue. One will recite their monologue whilst the other will be the volume button. They will indicate the volume by using their hand elevated. High hand indicates full volume, medium hand indicates normal speech volume and low hand means stage whisper. The young performer not only has to concentrate on the monologue and performance but on their partner's instructions.

TONGUE TWISTER

Individually or in pairs you are going to create a tongue twister. You should have chosen a first name for your character by now. Use the initial of your monologue character's first name to start the words. The tongue twister should include your character's:

- First Name
- What did she/he do?
- Where?
- When?
- Why?

FOR EXAMPLE:

Bob bought a bike in Brazil on his birthday because he was brave.

Suzie sang a song at the seaside on the sixth of September because she saw sunshine.

Once completed get each person to perform their tongue twister and the rest of the group can copy. Tongue twisters are a great way to explore vocally as they improve pronunciation and fluency. They can also help to improve accents by using alliteration, which is the repetition of one sound.

EMOTIONAL TABLEAU

A tableau is a theatrical technique in which performers freeze in positions that create a picture of an important moment. A tableau is all about great teamwork, telling a story, portraying a mood and ultimately expressing a single moment.

In groups choose a performer's monologue. The group will then create a tableau of a scene connected to that specific monologue.

Next: Add in movement before the freeze frame.
For example: *Walk around and on an agreed beat, movement or noise, freeze in position.*

Work through each monologue in the group.

GET IN THE HOT SEAT

Sit participants in a circle. Put one chair in the centre: 'The Hot Seat.'

One character enters the circle and sits in the hot seat.

Each member of the group will ask questions. The person in the hot seat has to answer the questions related to their character's backstory.

SELF-TAPES

Self-tapes are often used by casting directors to view audition pieces, allowing them to see if a performer is comfortable on camera and gauge their ability. Monologues are often used as part of this process.

Getting used to creating self-tapes is a great idea for young performers but is also an essential life skill in the modern digital age where video applications for everyday jobs are becoming more common. Mobile phones are often fine to use and give fantastic results for self-taping.

- Learn your lines and rehearse. Read any instructions that you may have been sent, thoroughly.
- Film in landscape, not portrait.
- Sit or stand depending on what feels comfortable/appropriate for the scene.
- Frame in a mid-close shot unless requested otherwise (chest to top of head).
- Make sure the camera is at eye-level and you are able to clearly see your full face.
- Sit or stand close to the phone to get the best sound. Ensure background noise is kept to a minimum.
- Light yourself properly. Use natural light if you can. Soft lighting is the best choice for a taped audition. Choose from a large light source which casts soft shadows. A small light source will cast a sharp shadow. The light source should be in front of you and not in shot. Don't sit with a window behind you. Sit facing the window.
- Try and find a plain background to film against – no furniture or distracting objects.
- Make sure your clothing is appropriate for the character.
- Only use props that are essential to the performance. Don't worry too much about action in the scene - concentrate on performance.
- Don't overthink. If you have done all the background work on your character it will show.
- Don't do too many takes. If you can't get it in three takes, take some time out, then try again.

At the beginning of the monologue introduce yourself with your name first, then add the monologue name.